OREGON,PORTLAND TRAVEL GUIDE 2025

For Outdoor Enthusiasts, History Buff,Foodie And High Spirit adventurer.

Brandie Coleman

Table of Contents

Chapter 1.Introduction

Welcome to Oregon

Greetings from Oregon

Upon disembarking from the aircraft and inhaling the clean, new air, I was immediately drawn to Oregon's untamed splendor. This state felt very much like a place where nature was still very much alive, with its towering mountains, untamed shoreline, and lush forests. I was enthralled by Oregon's varied scenery and limitless options for adventure from the moment I first visited. Whether it was Portland's exuberant energy or the expansive views along the Pacific Highway, I could not help but fall in love with Oregon's distinct charm.

Traveling along the well-known Route 101, which hugs the state's Pacific coast, is one of my favorite recollections. I had the impression that I was a part of something big and eternal because of the cliffs, thundering seas, and serene beaches. I recall stopping at a lookout to just stare in wonder at the ocean's infinite expanse while being grounded in the present by the sound of seabirds and the briny sea air. Experiences like these are what make Oregon more than simply a travel destination; it's a location where you may form lifelong connections with the natural world.

My exploration of Portland, with its eccentric districts and well-known culinary scene, offered me a taste of the cultural side of Oregon. The kindness of the people, who are always willing to share a smile or offer advice on the greatest nearby climb or secret coffee shop, was what impressed us. Every turn in Oregon appeared to reveal something new, be it a peaceful mountain route providing seclusion, a waterfall hidden away in the forest, or an unusual café giving up local goodies.

Oregon speaks to the spirit of adventure in all of us; it's more than just a destination. This state has a way of extending a warm welcome to everyone, regardless of whether you're coming back to see more. As it has inspired me, I hope this book will encourage you to set off on an unforgettable Oregon trip of your own.

Why Go to Oregon?

Whether you're an outdoor enthusiast, a history buff, a foodie, or just someone who likes to travel, Oregon has something to offer everyone. The state is one of the best-kept secrets in the nation because of its varied landscapes, vibrant culture, and easygoing charm. Here's why you should put Oregon on your travel itinerary:

Magnificent Natural Beauty: Oregon is a nature lover's paradise, with its untamed coast and high peaks of the Cascade Mountains. The state is home to amazing national parks including the Columbia River Gorge, which has an abundance of hiking routes and waterfalls, and Crater Lake, which has deep blue waters. Large forests and immaculate lakes make Oregon the ideal getaway for anyone looking for quiet and seclusion.

The Pacific Highway: Oregon boasts an incredibly beautiful stretch of the famous Pacific Coast Highway (Route 101). Beautiful ocean views, scenic beaches, and quaint coastal towns may all be found along the road that travels around the coast. It's ideal for an adventure-filled yet leisurely road vacation.

Outdoor Adventures: Oregon is a haven for intrepid travelers. The state's varied landscape makes it feasible to engage in whatever activity you choose, including hiking, biking, fishing, and kayaking. You can go surfing on the seashore, climb volcanic slopes, or explore old woods. Mount Hood provides some of the best snowboarding and skiing in the Pacific Northwest during the winter.

Scan the QR code

1. Open Camera: Launch your smartphone's camera app.

2. Position QR Code: Place the QR code within the camera's viewfinder.

3. Hold Steady: Keep the device steady for the camera to focus.

4. Wait for Scan: Wait for the code to be recognized.

5. Tap Notification: Follow the prompt to access the content.

Bright towns: Although Oregon is renowned for its breathtaking scenery, its towns are also worth a visit. The largest city in the state, Portland, is well known for its idiosyncratic appeal, craft beer scene, and farm-to-table culinary philosophy. The city offers a distinctive urban experience because of its creative vibe and emphasis on sustainability.

Wine Country: Known for its Pinot Noir, Oregon's Willamette Valley is one of the world's best wine areas. Wine lovers may visit more than 500 wineries while taking in breathtaking views of the vineyards and sampling some of the greatest wines in the nation.

Experiences with History and Culture: Oregon boasts a thriving culture and a wealth of natural history. Take a stroll through Portland's many art galleries, see Native American cultural sites, or explore quaint little communities. The state's progressive ideals combined with its dedication to historical preservation produce a distinctive cultural fabric.

Oregon is a food lover's paradise when it comes to local cuisine and craft beverages. The state's food scene places a strong emphasis on farm-to-table eating and uses only local, fresh ingredients. Portland is a foodie's dream come true with its James Beard Award-winning restaurants and food trucks. In addition, Oregon is well-known for its artisan coffee and beer scenes, with an abundance of breweries and cafes to discover.

Chapter 2. How to Travel to Oregon

Getting There by Air

One of the easiest ways to get to Oregon is by plane, as several airports offer both local and international flights. Portland International Airport (PDX) serves as the state's main airport, while connectivity to other regions of Oregon is provided by a number of regional airports.

Airport International in Portland (PDX)

Travelers entering Oregon primarily use Portland International Airport. Major American locations like Los Angeles, New York, Seattle, San Francisco, and Denver are among the many direct flights it offers. There are additional flights from places like Vancouver, Tokyo, and Amsterdam to other countries. PDX has received multiple honors for client satisfaction and is renowned for providing effective services.

- **Location**: Northeast Portland, roughly twelve miles from Portland's city center.

- **Terminals**: The primary terminal at PDX is split up into five concourses, A, B, C, D, and E. There are lots of stores, dining options, and travel services, making it simple to navigate.

- **Cost**: The average round-trip ticket price from major U.S. cities to Portland, depending on the season and airline availability, is $150 to $500. The price range for international travel is $600–1,200.

Airport Eugene (EUG)

Eugene Airport is a tiny, but well-connected, airport for flights to southern Oregon. With direct flights from major locations including Seattle, Denver, and San Francisco, it mostly serves domestic routes.

- The address is seven miles northwest of Eugene.

- **Terminals:** Passengers can easily navigate Eugene's sole terminal.

- **Cost**: Domestic round-trip tickets to Eugene start at $150 and go up to $400.

Medford's Rogue Valley International Airport (MFR)

The Rogue Valley, Ashland, Medford, and other nearby cities are served by Medford Airport, which is centrally located in southern Oregon. There are direct flights from Seattle, Denver, and San Francisco.

- 3 miles north of Medford is the location.

- **Terminals**: A single, highly efficient terminal.

- **Cost**: Round-trip tickets for domestic travel cost from $150 to $400.

Airport Redmond Municipal (RDM)

Direct flights from Denver, Salt Lake City, Los Angeles, and Portland are available to Redmond Airport for visitors to central Oregon, which includes Bend and Redmond.

- Two miles southeast of Redmond is the location.

- **Terminals**: One for domestic travel only.

- **Cost**: Round-trip airfares to Redmond start at $175 and go up to $350.

Oregon-Serving Airlines
Oregon airports are served by the following major airlines:

- Air Canada Delta

- Alaska Air

- Airlines Southwest

- United Carriers

- United States Air

With these choices, flying to Oregon is now among the quickest and most cost-effective options for visitors, particularly those who are traveling large distances. Costs will vary based on the time of year and season you book, but in general, Oregon has good connections to both domestic and foreign locations.

Traveling by car to Oregon
One of the most picturesque ways to see the Pacific Northwest is by car, as Oregon offers some of the most beautiful coastal, mountain, and woodland scenery. Oregon's well-maintained highways make for an unforgettable trip, whether you're coming from nearby states or farther away.

Well-travelled Paths to Oregon

via California (North Interstate 5).

Los Angeles, San Francisco, or Sacramento are good places to start.

Highway: The main north-south highway that links California and Oregon is Interstate 5 (I-5). This route begins in Southern California and travels through towns like Sacramento and Redding before entering Oregon in the vicinity of Ashland.

Landmarks: En route, you'll see the majestic Mount Shasta, drive through the Shasta-Trinity National Forest, and enter the Rogue Valley of Oregon. After entering Oregon, I-5 travels through towns like Eugene, Medford, Salem, and ultimately Portland.

Travel Time: 635 miles (10 hours) separate Portland from San Francisco, while roughly 960 miles (15 hours) separate Los Angeles from Portland.

Cost: The cost of gas for the journey is determined by how fuel-efficient your car is. Fuel for a car with a 25 mpg rating and an average price of $4.00 per gallon would cost between $150 and $200 for the drive from Los Angeles to Portland.

From I-5 South in Washington

Commencing Point: Spokane or Seattle

Route: The primary route from Seattle to Portland is Interstate 5 (I-5) South. After passing through Olympia and Vancouver, Washington, on the drive to Portland, you bridge the Columbia River.

Landmarks: The drive offers breathtaking vistas of the Cascade Mountains and includes views of Mount Rainier and Mount St. Helens.

Travel Time: Three hours and approximately 174 miles separate from Seattle and Portland.

Cost: Depending on how fuel-efficient your automobile is, the cost of gas for this trip might be anywhere from $30 to $50.

From Nevada (I-84 or US-395).

Starting Point: Las Vegas or Reno

Route: U.S. Route 395 or I-84 East will take you into Oregon if you're traveling from Nevada. Travel north from Reno via Susanville, California, and into Oregon close to Klamath Falls.

Landmarks: This route offers striking vistas of the mountains and desert while passing across the Great Basin and entering southern Oregon.

Driving Distance: 335 miles (6 hours) separate Reno, Nevada, from Bend, Oregon.

Cost: Gas for the drive from Reno would run you between $60 and $80.

from I-84 West in Idaho

Beginning Point: Boise

Route: The main route from Idaho into Oregon is Interstate 84 (I-84 West). As you get closer to Portland, you'll enter eastern Oregon and travel through the picturesque Columbia River Gorge.

Landmarks: Discover the breathtaking scenery of the Columbia River Gorge National Scenic Area, the Blue Mountains, and the Snake River along this route.

Boise to Portland is 430 miles away by car (7 hours).

Cost: This trip would cost between $70 and $90 in gas.

Rest Stops and Terminals
There are plenty of rest areas, petrol stations, and picturesque pull-offs along Oregon's roadways. Regular rest stops along interstate highways, such as I-5 and I-84, offer refreshments, fuel, and restrooms. Important pause points consist of:

Oak Grove Rest Area (close to Salem on I-5)

Rest Area Memaloose (I-84, close to the Gorge of the Columbia River)

Rest Area at French Prairie (I-5, close to Portland)

Extra Expenses

Tolls: The majority of Oregon's roadways are free of tolls, although there are a few bridges and routes that charge a small fee (around $2 to $3) for crossing them, such as the Bridge of the Gods in Cascade Locks.

Accommodations: Plan for overnight stays along the way at motels or hotels if your road journey necessitates them. The cost of lodging might vary from $80 to $150 per night, depending on the area.

Once in Oregon, scenic drives
When you get to Oregon, some of the most well-known picturesque roads to discover are:
The Pacific Coast Highway (US 101) offers breathtaking views of the Pacific Ocean, beaches, and sea cliffs as it winds down the Oregon coast.

The Columbia River Highway is a famed path that winds through the Columbia River Gorge and passes by picturesque vistas, hiking trails, and waterfalls.

Bus and Train Routes

If you want to unwind while travelling, taking the train or bus to Oregon is a beautiful and cozy option compared to driving there. Greyhound buses, which have several terminals and reasonable fares, and Amtrak trains provide convenient access from Oregon to major cities and surrounding states.

Oregon Train Routes

The main railroad operating in Oregon is Amtrak, which has a number of routes connecting the state to other regions of the Pacific Northwest and beyond. The most well-traveled Amtrak routes to Oregon consist of:

Coast Starlight (Oregon to Seattle via Los Angeles)

Route: Connecting major cities including Los Angeles, San Francisco, Portland, and Seattle, this route stretches along the

West Coast. It travels through the Willamette Valley and the Cascade Mountains, two beautiful regions.

Oregon has four terminals: Portland, Eugene, Albany, and Salem.

Get Time: It takes roughly 30 to 35 hours to get from Los Angeles to Portland.

Cost: The cost varies based on the time of year and the early booking. In coach class, a one-way ticket from Los Angeles to Portland can cost anything from $100 to $180.

Amtrak Cascades (from Eugene, OR to Vancouver, BC)

Route: Enjoy a leisurely journey through the Pacific Northwest with this regional service that links Eugene, Washington, Seattle, and Vancouver, British Columbia.

Oregon has four terminals: Portland, Eugene, Albany, and Salem.

Get Time: It takes around 3.5 hours to get from Seattle to Portland and 2 hours to travel from Eugene to Portland.

Cost: From Seattle to Portland, tickets range in price from $30 to $60. From Eugene, a trip to Portland usually costs between $20 and $40.

Empire Builder: Portland/Seattle to Chicago

line: This long-distance Amtrak line splits at Spokane, Washington, with one branch going to Portland and the other to Seattle, connecting Chicago to the Pacific Northwest.

Portland Union Station is one of Oregon's terminals.

Travel Time: It takes roughly 46–48 hours to complete the trip from Chicago to Portland.

Cost: A $150–$250 coach ticket will get you from Chicago to Portland.

Oregon Bus Routes
Greyhound and other regional bus services provide an extensive network connecting Oregon to other states and cities for people who would rather travel by bus.

Buses operated by Greyhound

Routes: Greyhound has several routes that connect Oregon with California, Washington, Idaho, and Nevada. Buses from Los Angeles, San Francisco, Seattle, and Boise are frequently routed to destinations like Portland, Eugene, and Medford.

Oregon's terminals include Salem, Medford, Eugene's Fifth Street Station, Portland's Union Station, and many regional stops.

Travel Time: It takes around 24 hours to travel by bus from Los Angeles to Portland, and it takes about 3.5 hours to travel from Seattle to Portland.

Price:
Tickets from Los Angeles to Portland cost between $90 and $120.

The fare from San Francisco to Portland is $60 to $100.

From Seattle to Portland: Generally, tickets cost between $15 and $35.

BoltBus

Routes: BoltBus connects Eugene, Portland, and Seattle with service throughout the West Coast.

Oregon has two terminals: Eugene (5th Street Station) and Portland (NW Station Way).

Get Time: It takes roughly 3.5 hours to get from Seattle to Portland.

Cost: Fares for a one-way ride from Seattle to Portland can start as low as $1 if reservations are made well in advance. On average, tickets cost between $10 and $20.

Bus FlixBus

Routes: FlixBus is a more recent, reasonably priced bus service that links Oregon with locations in California and the Pacific Northwest.

Terminals in Oregon: The primary FlixBus stops are in Eugene and Portland.

Travel Time: It takes around 3.5 hours from Seattle to Portland and 15 hours from San Francisco to Portland.

Cost: Depending on the route and how early you book, fares can range from $10 to $50, which is normally an inexpensive range.

Terminals

Amtrak and Greyhound's primary hub, Portland Union Station, is situated at 800 NW 6th Ave. in Portland. When arriving in the city by train or bus, passengers gather at this ancient station.

The Eugene 5th Street Station, at 433 Willamette St., is a major Amtrak Cascades and regional bus terminus.

The Salem Amtrak Station is at 500 13th St SE in Salem. It is used by Greyhound buses as well as Amtrak trains.

Extra Expenses

Food and Drink: You might want to buy meals or snacks for longer rail and bus trips. Amtrak offers dining cars and cafés where you can have meals for $5 to $20.

Fees for additional baggage: Greyhound and FlixBus have the ability to impose additional fees for each additional bag. These fees normally range from $15 to $20.

Chapter 3. Ideal Time to Go

Seasons and the Weather

Oregon's climate changes greatly depending on where and when you visit due to its varied landscape, which includes the high desert, the Pacific coastline, and the Cascade Mountains. To ensure you have the best possible trip to this breathtaking state, it is important to know the weather and seasons.

Springtime spans from March until May.

Weather: Oregon's springtime is pleasant yet erratic, with lots of rain showers. 50°F to 70°F (10°C to 21°C) is the usual temperature range, with warmer weather inland and colder temps at the shore.

What to Expect: When Oregon emerges from winter, its landscapes burst into life with vibrant wildflowers, verdant foliage, and snowmelt that powers the state's waterfalls. This time of year, the Willamette Valley—known for its wineries—is especially lovely.

Best Activities: Hiking, wine tasting, and visiting waterfalls like Multnomah Falls are all excellent throughout the spring. Rain, though, can make some outdoor activities more difficult.

Prices & Crowds: Spring is a quieter, more economical season to travel, with excellent lodging values due to a decrease in tourist traffic.

Summertime, from June to August

Weather: With warm, bright days and little rain, summer is the busiest travel season. Most places get temperatures between 70°F and 90°F (21°C and 32°C), with the coast experiencing somewhat colder temperatures between 60°F and 70°F (15°C and 21°C).

What to Expect: The ideal time of year for outdoor activities is now. Clear skies are perfect for hiking, camping, and car vacations along the picturesque Pacific Coast Highway throughout the entire state.

Best Activities: Take advantage of the many lakes and rivers for water sports, trek the Columbia River Gorge, explore Crater Lake National Park, and relax on the beaches along the Oregon Coast.

Summer is the most popular season, thus there are more people and more expensive lodging options, particularly in popular tourist destinations like Portland, Bend, and the coast.

Autumn (September through November)

Weather: Fall delivers crisp, bright days early in the season with increasing rain as November approaches. Temperatures range from 50°F to 75°F (10°C to 24°C). Across the state, the shifting leaves have added brilliant autumnal hues.

What to Expect: Fall is a beautiful time of year, particularly in the wine region and the surrounding woodlands. Many crops are also in harvest, so now is a fantastic time to sample local wine and vegetables.

Best Activities: Take a wine-tasting tour at a vineyard, hike through gorgeous fall foliage, and visit the Oregon Coast when the weather is still great but the crowds have thinned.

Prices and Crowds: Although early autumn is a popular time to visit, following Labor Day, there is a noticeable decline in both.

Winter, which lasts from December to February

Weather: The winters in Oregon vary a lot depending on where you live. Temperatures around the coast range from 40°F to 55°F (4°C to 13°C), although they can be stormy and damp. On the other hand, the mountains see high snowfall and 20s and 30s temperatures (-6 to 4°C).

What to Expect: Oregon's winter season, especially in the western portion of the state, is wet. But it's also the ideal season for Cascade snow sports.

Chapter 4. Examining the Pacific Highway in Oregon

An overview of Route 101

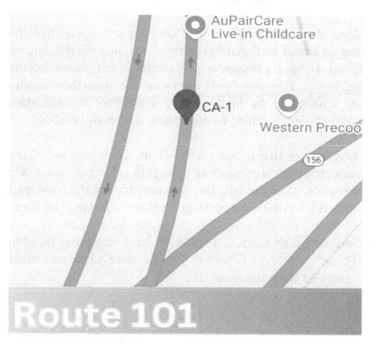

Scan the QR code

1. Open Camera: Launch your smartphone's camera app.
2. Position QR Code: Place the QR code within the camera's viewfinder.
3. Hold Steady: Keep the device steady for the camera to focus.
4. Wait for Scan: Wait for the code to be recognized.
5. Tap Notification: Follow the prompt to access the content.

One of the most picturesque journeys in the country is Route 101, popularly referred to as the Pacific Coast Highway, which stretches along the untamed and stunning Oregon coast. This well-known route, which offers breathtaking views of the ocean, tall cliffs, deep forests, and quaint coastal communities, stretches from the northern border with Washington to the southern edge close to California.

Along Route 101, visitors can discover attractions like the Oregon Dunes National Recreation Area, historic lighthouses dotted along the coast, and Cannon Beach, home of the well-known Haystack Rock. For those who enjoy the outdoors and adventure, the highway is a must-drive through state parks, charming fishing communities, and sandy beaches.

How to get there: Astoria, Newport, Coos Bay, and many more popular communities along the Oregon coast are accessible via Route 101. Heading west toward the coast, you can make it to the highway from Portland in just over an hour.

Cost: Although Route 101 is free to drive, there may be $5 to $15 per vehicle in entrance fees for state parks and other attractions along the route.

Top Attractions Along the Coast

There are many famous locations and undiscovered treasures along Oregon's Route 101 that provide the ideal fusion of adventure, history, and scenic beauty. The following places are a must-see:

The Astoria

- **Things to See and Do:** Start your seaside adventure at Astoria, the oldest American community west of the Rockies. Take in the expansive views from the Astoria

Column and discover the maritime history of the area by exploring the Columbia River Maritime Museum.

The Astoria Bridge, the Flavel House Museum, and Fort Stevens State Park are among the highlights.

Cannon Beach

- **Things to Explore**: Cannon Beach, well-known for its breathtaking shoreline and the recognizable Haystack Rock, is a photographer's paradise. Enjoy the little town's stores and art galleries while strolling along the beach at low tide to see tidal pools teeming with marine life.

  Highlights include Haystack Rock, Ecola State Park, and nearby art galleries.

As of Tillamook

- **Things to Do**: Take a tour and sample some of Oregon's best cheeses and ice cream at the Tillamook Creamery. Enjoy the scenic farmlands and pay a visit to the Tillamook Air Museum, which is housed in a former blimp hangar.

- **Points of interest**: Cape Meares Lighthouse, Tillamook Creamery, and Tillamook Air Museum.

Pacific City

- **Things to Do**: Pacific City, home to Cape Kiwanda, provides breathtaking views of the ocean, enormous dunes, and a more private seaside experience. Have a snack at Pelican Brewing, which is located on the beach, or watch dory boats take off from the shore.

Highlights include climbing dunes, Pelican Brewing, and Cape Kiwanda.

Newport

- **Things to See and Do:** There are several attractions in this busy seaside town, including the historic Yaquina Bay Lighthouse and the Oregon Coast Aquarium. Don't pass up the opportunity to explore the vibrant Bayfront, which is home to working fishing boats and sea lions, or to visit the Rogue Ales Brewery.

- **Points of interest**: Newport Historic Bayfront, Oregon Coast Aquarium, and Yaquina Head Lighthouse.

Oregon Dunes National Recreation Area and Florence

- **Things to Do**: The Oregon Dunes, a 40-mile expanse of enormous dunes ideal for hiking, sandboarding, and dune buggies, are accessible from Florence. It's also worthwhile to visit Florence's Old Town because of its distinctive stores and eateries.

  Highlights: Sea Lion Caves, Siuslaw River Bridge, and Sandboarding in the Dunes.

Bandon

- **Things to Explore**: Bandon is a more sedate coastal town, well-known for its pristine beaches and untamed rock formations. Take a stroll around the Coquille River Lighthouse or explore the Bandon Marsh National Wildlife Refuge.

  The Coquille River Lighthouse, Bandon Beach, and Bandon Dunes Golf Resort are among the highlights.

Boardman State Scenic Corridor Samuel H.

- **Things to Explore**: Some of Oregon's most stunning views may be found along this length of coastline. Visit the Arch Rock and Natural Bridges overlooks to take in the spectacular sea stacks and cliffs. Hikers and photographers will find bliss here.

  Highlights: Arch Rock, Hidden Beach, and Natural Bridges.

- **Cost**: The majority of the attractions along Route 101 are free, however, there may be a $5–$10 day-use fee at certain state parks. Visits to aquariums and the renting of dune buggy vehicles could incur additional fees.

Scenic Tour

While the Oregon Coast along Route 101 is breathtaking on its own, several picturesque detours let visitors explore the natural beauty and undiscovered treasures of the state in greater detail. These side trips result in beautiful scenery, secluded coves, and lesser-known activities that are well worth spending a little more time exploring.

Three Capes Recreational Path

- **Things to Explore**: The Three Capes Scenic Route, a detour off Route 101, passes through some of the most stunning coastal scenery. Cape Lookout, Cape Kiwanda, and Cape Meares are all included in the trip. Climb the dunes at Cape Kiwanda, stroll the paths at Cape Lookout for breathtaking views of the ocean, or explore the Cape Meares Lighthouse.

  Highlights include sandboarding at Cape Kiwanda, the Octopus Tree, Cape Lookout State Park, and the Cape Meares Lighthouse.

- **Price**: Free (state parks may charge a nominal parking fee).

National Park of Crater Lake

- **Things to Do**: Crater Lake National Park is a must-see for anybody interested in learning more about Oregon's volcanic past and its crystal-clear blue waters, even though it requires a sizable inland detour. The deepest lake in the US is Crater Lake, which was created in a volcanic crater. Take a boat trip to Wizard Island, go hiking, or take beautiful drives.

- The Cleetwood Cove Trail, Wizard Island, and Rim Drive are the highlights.

- **Price**: $30 for a seven-day pass per car.

Gorge of the Columbia River

- **Things to Explore**: Take a trip northeast to the Columbia River Gorge, which provides breathtaking views, cliffs, and towering waterfalls. Explore the Historic Columbia River Highway, renowned for its vistas and breathtaking scenery, trek along paths through lush forests and visit the famous Multnomah Falls.

- The Vista House, Latourell Falls, Horsetail Falls, and Multnomah Falls are the highlights.

- **Cost**: Free (some waterfalls may charge for parking).

Mount Hood

- **Things to Explore**: Mount Hood, another inland excursion, offers a striking contrast to the surrounding landscape with its snow-capped peaks and alpine lakes. In the summer, Mount Hood is a great way to get away from the coastal landscape, whether you're hiking or skiing. You can also go to Timberline Lodge, a historic property that was used to film *The Shining* and is well-known for its architecture.

  Highlights: Mount Hood National Forest, Timberline Lodge, and Trillium Lake.

- **Cost**: Free, though certain leisure areas including Timberline Lodge may have parking fees.

Amateur Wine Region: Willamette Valley

- **Things to Do**: The Willamette Valley in Oregon is a short inland excursion that is well-known for its world-class wines, especially its Pinot Noir. Savor local farm-to-table dining options, picturesque country drives, and wine tastings at several wineries. Ideal for taking a vacation from the seaside.

  Highlights: Beautiful vineyard tours, neighborhood artisan markets, and wine tastings at wineries.

- **Cost**: Admission is free; wine tastings run between $15 and $25 per person.

Silver Falls State Park

- **Things to Explore**: The well-known *Trail of Ten Falls*, a circular trail that winds through verdant woodland and behind breathtaking waterfalls, is located in Silver Falls State Park, east of Salem. It's a peaceful diversion that highlights the inland regions of Oregon's natural splendor.

  South Falls, Winter Falls, Canyon Trail, and North Falls are the highlights.

- **Price**: $5 per day for each vehicle.

Cascade Lakes and Elk Lake Scenic Byway

- **Things to Explore**: The Cascade Lakes Scenic Byway, which is close to Bend, offers breathtaking vistas of the mountains, glistening alpine lakes, and a never-ending list of outdoor activities. Enjoy the stunning views of the Cascade Range, go hiking on neighboring trails, or go kayaking on Elk Lake.

- **Highlights**: Mount Bachelor, Lava Lake, Sparks Lake, and Elk Lake.

- **Price**: Free (parking may be charged at some lake access locations).

- **Pro Tip**: While many of these picturesque detours are open all year round, some are best experienced in the summer when the roads are free of snow, such as Crater Lake and Mount Hood. Make sure to always verify the state of the roads before planning a diversion!

Chapter 5. Best Places to Go

The City of Roses, Portland

Known as the "City of Roses," Portland, Oregon, is a dynamic and diversified city that offers a blend of natural beauty, a broad culture, and unique attractions. This city, which is renowned for its lovely rose gardens, green areas, and vibrant food and arts scene, is tucked away in the shadow of Mount Hood.

Things to Look Into:

- **International Rose Test Garden**: With over 10,000 rose bushes and breathtaking vistas of the city and Mount Hood, this garden is a must-see for anybody who enjoys flowers. It costs nothing to enter.

- **Portland Japanese Garden**: A peaceful haven in the center of the city, this garden is one of the most authentic Japanese gardens outside of Japan. Adults must pay $19.95 to enter.

- **Pittock Mansion**: Discover the historic residence of Henry Pittock, one of Portland's early pioneers, which offers breathtaking city views. Adults must pay $12 to enter.

- **Powell's City of Books**: The biggest independent bookshop in the world is a sanctuary for readers.

Explore at your leisure, however you might be tempted to purchase a few trinkets.

- **Food Carts and Brewers**: Portland is well-known for both its artisan brewers and food cart scene. Savor regional cuisine and beverages while exploring the city.

Price:

- **Lodging**: Hotel rates range from $120 to $200 per night for mid-range accommodations.

- **Dining**: Budget $10 to $15 for food carts and $20 to $40 for restaurants.

- **Public Transportation**: For $5 per person, a day pass for the Portland TriMet public transportation system allows unlimited trips on buses, the MAX Light Rail, and streetcars.

How to Travel There:

- **By Air**: Portland International Airport (PDX) has excellent air transportation connections to both local and foreign locations. The airport is located approximately 12 miles from downtown, yet it only takes around 38 minutes to get to the city center on the MAX Light Rail, which costs $2.60 one way.

- **By Train**: Union Station, the train station, is in downtown Portland. Amtrak provides services in the city.

- **By Road**: Interstate 5 makes it simple to travel from Portland to cities in California and Washington.

Bend: Nature Exploration in Central Oregon

Bend, in Central Oregon, is a haven for outdoor enthusiasts. Bend, well-known for its sunny days, untamed scenery, and proximity to mountains, rivers, and forests, provides both outdoor enthusiasts and those seeking adventure with a year-round playground.

Things to Look Into:

- **Deschutes River**: This picturesque river winds through the center of Bend and is great for kayaking, paddleboarding, and tubing. Equipment rentals are available, with half-day rentals starting at about $25.

- **Smith Rock State Park**: This park is a must-see because of its breathtaking views, hiking trails, and rock-climbing reputation. Each car costs $5 to enter.

- **Mount Bachelor**: During the winter, Mt. Bachelor is a well-known spot for snowboarding and skiing. The daily cost of lift tickets is about $109. Summertime brings mountain biking and breathtaking chairlift excursions to the area.

- **Deschutes National Forest**: Take a hike or go mountain biking through routes that pass through verdant forests and lead to alpine lakes and waterfalls. Access to many trails is free.

- **Breweries**: There are numerous craft breweries located in Bend. Go on an exploration of the Bend Ale Trail and enjoy some locally brewed beer. Prices can vary, but a pint should cost between $5 and $8.

Price:

- **Lodging**: The cost of a room varies from $100 to $250 a night, contingent on the time of year and the distance from outdoor attractions.

- **Outdoor Rentals**: The cost of renting a kayak or paddleboard is $25, while the cost of renting a ski or snowboard in the winter is approximately $45 per day.

- **Dining**: $12 to $30 per person is the pricing range for the substantial meals served at local restaurants.

How to Travel There:

- **By Air:** Redmond Municipal Airport (RDM), located roughly 17 miles north of the city, serves Bend. It takes around 30 minutes to drive from the airport to Bend; shuttle services and vehicle rentals are offered.

- **By Road**: It takes roughly three hours (160 miles) to get there from Portland using U.S. Highway 26 and U.S. Route 97, which provides breathtaking vistas of the Cascade Mountains as you travel.

Eugene: A Cultural and Natural University Town

The lively university town of Eugene, Oregon, is situated between the Pacific coast and the Cascade Mountains. Eugene, home of the University of Oregon, is well-known for its diverse range of outdoor pursuits, cultural attractions, and flourishing arts scene. It also provides a distinctive fusion of nature and culture.

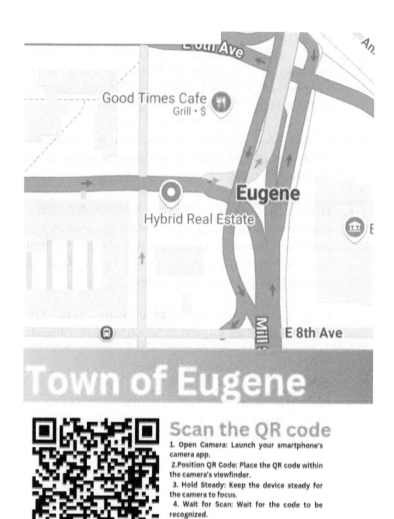

Town of Eugene

Scan the QR code

1. **Open Camera:** Launch your smartphone's camera app.

2. **Position QR Code:** Place the QR code within the camera's viewfinder.

3. **Hold Steady:** Keep the device steady for the camera to focus.

4. **Wait for Scan:** Wait for the code to be recognized.

5. **Tap Notification:** Follow the prompt to access the content.

Things to Look Into:

- **University of Oregon**: This stunning campus, which combines modern amenities with historic buildings, is a must-see. The entrance charge to the campus's Museum of Natural and Cultural History is approximately $6.

- **Owen Rose Garden**: Surrounded by more than 4,500 rose bushes, this free garden close to downtown is ideal for a stroll.

- **Hiking at Spencer Butte**: Spencer Butte is a popular hiking destination with breathtaking panoramic views of Eugene, just a short drive from the city center. It's a terrific site to take in Oregon's natural splendor, and entry is free.

- **Hult Center for the Performing Arts**: This cultural center in Eugene is home to plays, concerts, and art exhibits. Although they vary, tickets typically cost between $20 and $60.

- **Saturday Market**: Experience local food, live music, and crafts at this bustling downtown market, which is open from April through November. Prices change based on what you buy.

Price:

- **Lodging**: Nightly rates for hotels and guesthouses in Eugene range from $90 to $200.

- **Dining**: There are many different alternatives available at local restaurants, with meals costing anything from $10 to $25 per person.

- **Activities**: Admission to museums and shows at the Hult Center may cost anything from $6 to $60, although the majority of outdoor activities are free.

How to Travel There:

- **By Air**: The distance from the downtown area to Eugene Airport (EUG) is roughly 10 kilometers. From the airport, a taxi or shuttle takes 15 to 20 minutes and costs $20 to $30.

- **By Road**: Eugene may be reached easily and picturesquely by Interstate 5 (I-5) through the Willamette Valley, about an hour's drive south of Portland.

- **By Train/Bus:** As an alternative to driving, Eugene is served by Amtrak's Coast Starlight line and the Greyhound bus. From Portland, train rates start at about $35.

Ashland: The Oregon Shakespeare Festival and the Arts

The picturesque town of Ashland, Oregon, is well-known for its thriving arts scene, especially for the internationally recognized Oregon Shakespeare Festival (OSF), which attracts tourists from all over the world. Ashland, tucked away in the Siskiyou Mountains' foothills, combines breathtaking scenery with a vibrant cultural scene.

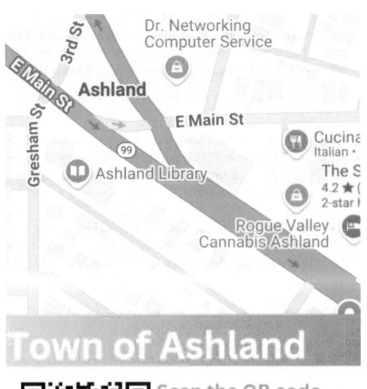

Town of Ashland

Scan the QR code

1. Open Camera: Launch your smartphone's camera app.
2. Position QR Code: Place the QR code within the camera's viewfinder.
3. Hold Steady: Keep the device steady for the camera to focus.
4. Wait for Scan: Wait for the code to be recognized.
5. Tap Notification: Follow the prompt to access the content.

Things to Look Into:

- **Oregon Shakespeare** Festival: The OSF presents several plays, including both modern and traditional Shakespearean pieces, from February to October.

Three theaters host performances, one of which is the outdoor Allen Elizabethan Theatre. Ticket prices vary from $40 to $140 based on the performance and location.

Lithia Park is a 93-acre park ideal for strolling either before or after a performance. Along Ashland Creek, there are walking routes, duck ponds, and gardens. The park is free to enter.

- **Downtown Ashland**: Take a tour of Main Street's quaint shops, galleries, and cafés. Handmade goods and artwork are available at the Ashland Art Center and nearby stores.

- **ScienceWorks Hands-On Museum**: This interactive museum with a science theme is excellent for families. Adult admission is $10, while children's admission is $8.

- **Mount Ashland**: Skiing and snowboarding are available at the Mount Ashland Ski Area during the winter. Depending on age and the time of year, lift tickets range in price from $30 to $60.

Price:

- **Lodging**: Ashland offers a variety of hotel options, from low-cost hotels that cost about $90 per night to upscale boutique inns that cost $250 or more.

- **Dining**: At neighborhood eateries, a meal can cost $10 for casual fare or more at fancy dining locations.

- **Activities**: Tickets for the Oregon Shakespeare Festival might cost anywhere from $40 to $140, but outdoor pursuits like touring Lithia Park are free.

How to Travel There:

- **By Air**: Rogue Valley International-Medford Airport (MFR), which is roughly 20 minutes from Ashland, is the closest. From the airport, a taxi fare to Ashland is approximately $30.

- **Via Car:** Ashland is about four hours south of Portland and five hours north of San Francisco, situated right off Interstate 5. The journey through the Rogue Valley is breathtaking.

- **By Bus/Train**: You may take a bus or shuttle to Ashland from nearby Medford, which is served by Amtrak's train services. Greyhound and other bus companies connect to Medford as well; tickets start at approximately $30.

Chapter 6. Outdoor Adventures

Oregon Hiking: Trails for All Skill Levels

Hiking paths in Oregon are among the most beautiful and varied in the nation, appealing to hikers of all skill levels. For both novice and experienced hikers, Oregon's trails offer an amazing experience, ranging from verdant forests to dramatic coastal cliffs, snow-capped summits, and high desert vistas.

Novice Routes:

- **Silver Falls State Park (Trail of Ten Falls):** This 7.2-mile circle is one of Oregon's most well-known waterfall treks, and it's close to Salem. Ten stunning waterfalls may be seen along the somewhat easy trek, some of which even go below the falls. It costs $5 to park, but admission is free.

- **Hoyt Arboretum (Portland):** This urban trail system meanders through a variety of tree species, making it ideal for families and novices. There are 12 kilometers of easily navigable paths with small loops. There is no charge, although parking is $2 per hour.

Trails in the Middle:

- **Tom, Dick, and Harry Mountain (Mount Hood):** Enjoy stunning vistas of the Cascade Range on this 9-mile out-and-back trek close to Mount Hood. Although the trek gains around 1,700 feet in height, most intermediate hikers can handle it. Although parking requires a Northwest Forest Pass ($5 per day), there is no admission charge.

- **Cape Lookout (Oregon Coast):** This 5-mile hike offers breathtaking views of the Pacific Ocean as it takes you out onto a picturesque coastal point. The trail's little elevation climb makes it quite difficult. At the trailhead, parking costs $5.

Trails for Experts:

- **South Sister**: Located in Central Oregon, this 12-mile path is an excellent choice for those seeking a strenuous hike. Hikers ascend more than 4,900 feet to the summit of South Sister, the third-highest peak in the state. The hike is challenging, but the payoff is a panoramic vista of the Cascades. Parking passes are needed, but admission is free.

- **Eagle Creek (Columbia River Gorge):** This strenuous trek is 12 miles in total and is well-known for its cliffside pathways and waterfalls, which include the well-known Tunnel Falls. It is best suited for more experienced hikers due to its high drop-offs. Although parking is free, a Northwest Forest Pass ($5 per day) is needed.

Summary of Costs:

- Daily parking costs vary from $5 to $10.

- A Northwest Forest Pass is available for $5 per day or $30 per year.

For most treks, trail entrance is free; however, certain locations need a recreation pass.

- The cost of gear (hiking boots, day packs, etc.) varies, but essentials can be rented for $20 to $40 per day.

State and National Parks

There are a staggering number of national and state parks in Oregon that showcase the state's varied landscapes, which range from serene lakes and vast forests to rocky coastlines and high mountains. Visitors can hike, camp, fish, and take in the natural splendor of the Pacific Northwest in these parks.

National Park of Crater Lake

The deepest lake in the country and the focal point of Oregon's national parks, Crater Lake is known for its breathtaking blue hue. Hiking routes, boat cruises to Wizard Island, and picturesque lakeside drives are all available at the park. It is a place to go cross-country skiing and snowshoeing in the winter.

- **Price**: $35 for each car (good for seven days); $55 for an annual pass.

- **Mazama Campground**: $21–$31 per night (summer only).

The National Forest of Mount Hood

Encircling the highest point in Oregon, Mount Hood National Forest provides year-round outdoor activities such as hiking and camping in the summer and skiing and snowboarding in the winter. Thousands of people visit popular paths like the Timberline Trail and enjoy the views from Trillium Lake.

- **Cost**: Parking at numerous trailheads requires a Northwest Forest Pass, which costs $5 per day or $30 annually.

- **Camping**: In developed campgrounds, costs $20 to $30 per night.

Silver Falls State Park
Often referred to as the "crown jewel" of state parks in Oregon, Silver Falls is home to the well-known Trail of Ten Falls, a lush, forested trail that allows hikers to pass behind multiple waterfalls. It's a fantastic location for camping, picnics, and animal observation.

- **Price**: $5 for parking each day.

- **Camping**: Cabin rents cost $52 per night, while tent and RV sites cost between $22 and $31.

Smith Rock State Park
For those who enjoy the great outdoors and rock climbing, this state park is legendary. Smith Rock, which is in Central Oregon, provides an opportunity to see golden eagles and other animals, as well as world-class climbing and picturesque hiking paths. The Misery Ridge Trail in the park provides amazing views of the surrounding peaks and the Crooked River.

- **Price**: $5 for parking each day.

- Camping at the walk-in Bivouac Campground is $8 per person.

Gorge of the Columbia River National Scenic Area
The 620-foot Multnomah Falls, the highest in Oregon, is one of the many magnificent waterfalls in the Columbia River Gorge that are well-known. In addition, windsurfing, hiking paths, and picturesque drives with expansive vistas of the Columbia River are well-known in the area.

- **Cost**: A Northwest Forest Pass ($5 per day) is required for parking at several popular locations, and $2 per vehicle may be charged during high season for reservations at Multnomah Falls.

- Campsites in the area cost $20 to $30 per night.

National Recreation Area of the Oregon Dunes
The Oregon Dunes, which stretches 500 feet above sea level along the southern Oregon coast, offer a strange scene of dunes. Along with enjoying the neighboring beaches, visitors can explore the dunes on foot, via ATV, or on a guided trip.

- **Cost**: $5 per day for parking in various locations.

- **Camping**: at developed campgrounds, $22-$31 per night.

Cape Perpetua Nature Reserve
Thor's Well, Devil's Churn, and the Cape Perpetua Overlook are among the striking coastline vistas seen on this portion of the Siuslaw National Forest, Cape Perpetua. For breathtaking views, hikers can follow untamed ocean cliffs or old woodlands.

- **Cost**: Northwest Forest Pass or $5 day-use parking fee.

- Camping at Cape Perpetua Campground is $22 to $28 per night.

An overview of the expenses

- **Day-use fees**: $5 per car for the majority of national forest and state parks.

- **Northwest Forest Pass**: $30 for an annual pass, or $5 per day.

- **Crater Lake National Park Entrance**: $30 per vehicle (7 days).

- **Camping**: Most campgrounds cost between $20 and $30 per night, with basic sites costing $8 and cabins costing $52.

Waterfalls: From Hidden Gems to Multnomah Falls

Beautiful waterfalls can be found in both easily accessible and off-the-beaten-path locales in Oregon, which is well known for them. For those who enjoy the outdoors and breathtaking scenery, Oregon's waterfalls—which range from the well-known Multnomah Falls in the Columbia River Gorge to lesser-known hidden gems—must be seen.

The Multnomah Falls

Multnomah Falls, the most well-known waterfall in Oregon, is a magnificent spectacle that plunges 620 feet from the surrounding rocks. The tallest waterfall in the state, it's conveniently accessible from Portland and situated in the Columbia River Gorge. Hikers can ascend the trail to the top for expansive views, or they can watch the falls from a picturesque bridge.

- **Cost**: $2 timed reservation fee from May through September, when it's busiest; parking may additionally need a $30 yearly pass or a $5 daily Northwest Forest Pass.

Silver Falls State Park

Silver Falls State Park, the location of the well-known Trail of Ten Falls, provides an immersive waterfall experience. You may hike behind South Falls and North Falls, among other falls. Hikers and photographers love this verdant forest park.

- **Price**: $5 for parking each day.

- The 7.2-mile Trail of Ten Falls loop.

Toketee Waterfall

Nestled among basalt columns, Toketee Falls is a hidden jewel situated in the Umpqua National Forest. It is a 113-foot waterfall that falls in two stages. For those who enjoy the outdoors, the short and easily navigable trail to the falls is an ideal destination in Southern Oregon.

- **Cost**: No admission cost; parking is free.

Latourell Waterfall

Latourell Falls, another treasure in the Columbia River Gorge, is renowned for its remarkable columnar basalt formations and plunges 249 feet in a single tumble. Guy W. Talbot State Park is home to the waterfall, and the hike to its base is somewhat easy and quick.

- **Cost**: Northwest Forest Pass or $5 parking fee.

Salt Creek Waterfall

At 286 feet, Salt Creek Falls, the second-tallest waterfall in Oregon, is situated in the Cascade Mountains. An easy route leads nearer to the falls, and the viewing platform offers an excellent viewpoint. Particularly when encircled by snow in the winter, this waterfall is a hidden gem.

- **Cost**: Northwest Forest Pass or $5 parking fee.

The Abiqua Falls

It takes a little adventure to get to Abiqua Falls, which is close to Scotts Mills and is one of the state's most remote waterfalls. The journey to the falls requires climbing over rocks and a rocky path to the trailhead, but the 92-foot waterfall surrounded by basalt cliffs is well worth the effort.

- **Cost**: Free; but, because of the difficult driving conditions, parking may be restricted.

The Tamanawas Falls

Tamanawas Falls is a hidden gem in the Mount Hood National Forest, accessible via a 3.5-mile round-trip journey past verdant forests and a bubbling brook. At the end of the hike, there's a lovely 110-foot waterfall.

- **Cost**: Northwest Forest Pass or $5 parking fee.

An overview of the expenses

- **Parking and entry fees**: $5 per car for the majority of parks and locations.

- The Northwest Forest Pass costs $5 daily or $30 a year.

- During high season, Multnomah Falls Reservation Fee: $2.

National Park of Crater Lake

A stunning gem located in Southern Oregon, Crater Lake National Park is well-known for its deep blue lake that was created when a volcano fell. The focal point of the park, Crater Lake, is home to a variety of outdoor activities, stunning views, and the clearest lake in the US.

Things to Look Into

- **Crater Lake:** The main draw of the park, renowned for its strikingly clear and vivid blue color. Numerous picturesque vantage spots, such as Watchman Peak and Rim Village, offer views of the lake.

- **Rim Drive**: A scenic 33-mile loop that encircles the lake. The beauty of the lake can be appreciated and photographs taken in several beautiful spots and pullouts.

- **Wizard Island**: A lakeside volcanic cinder cone that is accessible by boat cruises. It's an excellent place to explore and go trekking.

- **Hiking Trails**: routes include the Garfield Peak Trail, which provides sweeping views of the surrounding area, and the Cleetwood Cove Trail, which goes to the lake's coast.

How to Travel There

- **By Car**: US access is possible. Route 62. Medford, Oregon, is approximately two hours drive from the park.

- **By Air**: Rogue Valley International-Medford Airport, the closest major airport, is located in Medford and is about 85 miles away from the park. To go to Crater Lake from there, rent a car.

Price

$25 per car or $15 per person for those coming on foot or bicycle is the entrance fee. This charge is good for seven days in a row.

- **Annual Pass**: The Crater Lake National Park Annual Pass costs $50 and is good for a year after it is purchased.

Chapter 7. The Coast of Oregon

Beaches to Discover

Beach by the Sea

Popular coastal attraction Seaside Beach is situated in Seaside, Oregon, and is well-known for its wide sandy beach and colorful boardwalk. This beach provides chances for family fun, relaxation, and picturesque vistas, making it a quintessential Pacific Northwest beach experience.

Things to Look Into

- **The Promenade**: A 1.5-mile promenade that runs parallel to the beach and is ideal for bicycling, strolling, and taking in views of the ocean.

- **Seaside Aquarium**: Ideal for families interested in marine life, this aquarium is close to the beach.

- **Historic Carousel**: A quaint carousel on the boardwalk with intricate carvings.

- **Beach Activities**: Picnicking, swimming, and beachcombing. Beach bonfires and kite flying are seasonal hobbies.

How to Travel There

- **By Car**: Seaside Beach is conveniently located near U.S. Route 101. Portland, Oregon is roughly 90 miles away, or about a 1.5-hour drive.

- **By Bus**: There are a few routes from Portland that connect to Seaside via limited bus services.

Price

- **Parking**: There are public lots and street parking accessible. The majority of parking alternatives have a minor daily fee, usually $5.

- Beach Entry is Free.

The Newport Beach

Newport, Oregon is home to Newport Beach, a charming seaside resort. This beach, which is well-known for its untamed beauty, marine life, and quaint seaside ambiance, provides a variety of visiting activities.

Things to Look Into

- **Yaquina Head Outstanding Natural Area**: Known for its famous lighthouse, tide pools, and breathtaking views.

  The Oregon Coast Aquarium, as well as boutiques and seafood restaurants, may be found along Newport's historic bayfront.

- **Agate Beach**: A more sedate location noted for its agate stones and picturesque vistas.

- **Beach Activities**: swimming, tidal pool exploration, and beachcombing.

How to Travel There

- **By Car**: You may get to Newport Beach using U.S. Route 101. Portland, Oregon is roughly 130 miles away, or about a 2.5-hour travel.

- **By Bus**: Portland has a limited number of bus services; however, connections could be necessary.

Price

- **Parking**: There are several $5 to $10 daily public parking lots close to the beach.

- Beach Entry is Free.

Beach at Lincoln City
Manzanita Beach

Observing Wildlife and Whales

The two most popular things to do in Oregon are wildlife and whale watching, which provide exceptional chances to see the state's varied wildlife and stunning marine life.

Observing Wildlife

Things to Look Into:

- **Wildlife of the Pacific Northwest**: Contains bald eagles, deer, elk, black bears, and other bird species.

- The Willamette Valley is the best place to see migratory birds, while Smith Rock State Park is the best place to see raptors.

Price:

- Park-specific entrance fees range from $5 to $15.

- **Guided Tours**: Depending on the length and location of the tour, prices typically range from $50 to $150 per person.

Observing Whales

Things to Look Into:

- **Gray Whales**: From December to March, these animals migrate along the Oregon coast.

- **Seasonal Tours**: Offered in communities like Newport and Depoe Bay.

Price:

- **Tour Fees**: For a two- to four-hour expedition, whale-watching tours typically cost $60 to $100 per person.

- **Parking and Extras**: Optional tips and additional parking fees.

Chapter 8. Wine Country & Breweries

Discovering the Wine Region of Willamette Valley

Things to Look Into:

- **Vineyards & Wineries**: The Willamette Valley, known for its Pinot Noir, is home to more than 500 wineries. Carlton, McMinnville, and Dundee Hills are notable localities.

- **Tasting Rooms**: At wineries like Domaine Serene, Archery Summit, and Penner-Ash Wine Cellars, take advantage of guided tastings and tours.

- **Scenic Drives**: Particularly along Highway 99W and the Chehalem Mountain Wine Trail, the valley's undulating hills and charming vineyards make for a gorgeous backdrop for drives.

Price:

- **Wine tastings**: Usually cost between $10 and $25 per person and are frequently redeemed with a purchase.

- **Tours**: Depending on the duration and inclusions, guided tours and tastings normally run between $50 and $150 per person.

Oregon's Culture of Craft Beer

Oregon is a major center for craft beer in the US, with inventive brews, a thriving brewery environment, and a passionate beer culture. Hundreds of craft brewers that offer a wide variety of distinctive beer varieties may be found around the state.

Important Points to Note:

- **Portland**: Known for being the core of Oregon's craft beer scene, Portland is home to a large number of breweries, including well-known brands like Hair of the Dog, Bridgeport Brewing, and Deschutes Brewery. Along with a thriving beer scene, the city is home to numerous taprooms, brewpubs, and beer festivals.

- **Bend**: Known for having a high number of breweries in its population, this city is home to well-known establishments including 10 Barrel Brewing Co., Deschutes Brewery, and Boneyard Beer.

- **Eugene**: Known for the variety of its craft beers, Eugene is home to several breweries, including Viking Braggot Company, Oakshire Brewing, and Ninkasi Brewing Company.

Price:

- **Beer Tastings**: A flight of tiny samples usually costs between $5 and $10.

- **Pints**: Depending on the brewery and type of beer, they typically cost $4 to $7.

- **Brewery Tours**: Usually costing between $10 and $25, guided tours include samples.

Chapter 9. Special Natural Wonders

Hills with Paint

One of the three sections of eastern Oregon's John Day Fossil Beds National Monument is the Painted Hills. They are well known for the gorgeous, multicoloured sedimentary rock strata that they have, which produce a vivid, striped environment. Due to the distinct mineral deposits in the soil, the colors vary from rich reds and oranges to delicate yellows and browns. The landscape, which features fossils from the late Miocene era, is not only visually arresting but also rich in paleontological history.

Things to Look Into:

- **Vibrant Stripes**: The Painted Hills are mostly recognized for their layered, eye-catching hues. The colors are at their most intense around dawn and dusk.

- Walking Trails: Take a stroll along some of the trails, like the Leaf Hill Trail and the Painted Cove Trail, which provide up-close looks at the rock formations and the surrounding area.

- **Interpretive Center**: Discover the region's fossils and geology with educational exhibits and displays.

How to Travel There:

- **Location**: In Oregon, The Painted Hills are close to the town of Mitchell.

- **Directions**: Travel US-26 E to US-97 S from Portland. Next, take OR-207 S to the intersection of OR-26 E. Proceed on OR-26 E to the entrance of Painted Hills.

- **Travel Time**: It takes roughly 3.5 to 4 hours to drive from Portland to the Painted Hills.

Price:

- **Entrance cost**: There is a $15 minimal cost per vehicle to enter the John Day Fossil Beds National Monument. This fee is good for all monument units and is valid for seven days.

Mount Hood

Oregon's highest peak, Mount Hood, rises to 11,240 feet (3,426 meters). Located in the Cascade Range, this famous stratovolcano is a year-round favorite among outdoor enthusiasts. Mount Hood, which is well-known for its snow-capped peaks and gorgeous surroundings, provides opportunities for hiking, climbing, snowboarding, and skiing. The surroundings are home to a variety of environments, such as verdant woods and mountain meadows.

Things to Look Into:

- **Skiing and snowboarding**: Timberline Lodge and Mount Hood Meadows are two of Mount Hood's well-known ski resorts. This place offers excellent winter activities on terrain suitable for every skill level.

- **Hiking Trails**: The Mirror Lake Trail, which provides breathtaking views of the summit, and the Timberline Trail, which encircles the mountain, are two well-liked hiking routes.

- **Historic Timberline Lodge**: Situated at 5,960 feet (1,819 meters) above sea level, this lodge offers lodging and eating options accompanied by stunning mountain views.

- **Glaciers and Summits**: Mount Hood provides climbing routes, such as the well-liked South Route, to the summit for skilled climbers.

How to Travel There:

- **Location**: Portland, Oregon is 50 miles (or 80 kilometres) east of Mount Hood.

- **Directions**: Travel directly to the Mount Hood area on US-26 E from Portland. It takes roughly 1.5 to 2 hours to drive to Timberline Lodge, which is a popular starting place.

- **Travel Time**: Depending on the weather and road conditions, the travel from Portland to Mount Hood typically takes 1.5 to 2 hours.

Gorge of the Columbia River
The gorgeous 80-mile (129-kilometer) Columbia River Gorge is a canyon formed by the Columbia River that separates

Oregon and Washington. The Gorge, well-known for its breathtaking waterfalls, verdant forests, and sheer cliffs, provides an amazing backdrop for outdoor pursuits and picturesque vistas. The largest waterfall in Oregon, Multnomah Falls, and the picturesque vistas along the Historic Columbia River Highway are among the main draws.

Things to Look Into:

- **Multnomah Falls**: This 620-foot (189-meter) cascade, the largest in Oregon, is a must-see. It has a footbridge for viewing and a lovely location.

- **Hiking Trails**: Well-liked trails for hiking include the Angel's Rest Trail, which offers expansive views of the Gorge, and the Eagle Creek Trail, which has beautiful waterfalls.

- **Vista House**: This historic viewpoint at Crown Point is an excellent place to take pictures and offers expansive views of the Columbia River Gorge.

- **Waterfalls**: In addition to Multnomah Falls, Bridal Veil Falls, Horsetail Falls, and Latourell Falls are noteworthy waterfalls.

How to Travel There:

- **Location**: Portland, Oregon is approximately 30 miles (48 kilometers) east of the Columbia River Gorge.

- **Directions**: Travel the Interstate 84 highway (I-84 E) south of Portland, following the Columbia River

Gorge. Take US-14 through Washington State to reach the northern side.

- **Travel Time**: Depending on traffic and the exact location inside the Gorge, the travel from Portland to the Gorge typically takes between 30 and 45 minutes.

Chapter 10. Dining and Food

Yummie Oregon Recipes

The Dungeness Crab

The Pacific Northwest's highly valued seafood, Dungeness crab, is renowned for its delicate flavor and sweet, luscious meat. It's usually eaten boiling, steamed, or in recipes like chowder and crab cakes. A pound of fresh Dungeness crab typically costs $20 to $30, depending on the time of year and the state of the market.

Pie with Marionberries

A traditional Oregon treat, marionberry pie is created from marionberries, a tart and delicious hybrid berry that originated in Oregon. The pie has a sweet, mildly tart berry filling inside a flaky crust. At neighborhood bakeries or restaurants, a slice usually costs between $4 and $7, but the price of an entire pie can vary from $20 to $30, based on its size and quality.

Salmon with Smoke

In Oregon, smoked salmon is highly prized for its delicate texture and deep, smoky flavor. It is frequently eaten as an appetizer or as a side dish with salads and cream cheese on bagels. A pound of smoked salmon can cost anywhere from $15 to $30, depending on where it comes from and how it is prepared.

Tilapia from Oregon

Freshwater tilapia from Oregon is prized for its crisp, flaky texture and mild flavor. It can be pan-seared, roasted, or grilled, which makes it a flexible choice for a variety of recipes.

Oregon tilapia typically costs $10 to $20 per pound, depending on where and how fresh it is bought.

The Greatest Food Carts, Cafés, and Restaurants

Eatery

Portland's Le Pigeon

In Portland's Eastside, there's a well-known French-inspired bistro called Le Pigeon. The restaurant is well-known for both its creative menu and its warm, welcoming ambiance. Roasted lamb and profiteroles with foie gras are two of the restaurant's signature dishes.

- **Cost**: $50 to $75 per person (drinks and tip not included; appetizers, entrée, and dessert included).

- **How to Get There:** 738 E Burnside St, Portland, OR 97214 is the address. Take the Blue, Green, or Red lines of the MAX Light Rail from downtown Portland to the Burnside Bridge stop. From there, stroll east for about ten minutes. As an alternative, you can get from downtown in around five minutes by taxi or ridesharing.

Portland's Nostrana

Nostrana is a lively Italian restaurant that specializes in using foods that are produced locally and following classic Italian recipes. Wood-fired pizzas, homemade pasta, and a selection of antipasti are all offered on the menu. The eatery is renowned for its friendly service and cozy ambiance.

- **Cost**: $40 to $60 per person, which includes a drink, an entrée, and maybe a shared starter or dessert.

- **Directions**: 1401 SE Morrison St, Portland, OR 97214 is the address. You may walk for about ten minutes east after taking the Green or Orange lines of the MAX Light Rail from downtown Portland to the Morrison/SW 3rd stop. Alternatively, a cab or rideshare will take roughly 5 minutes from downtown.

Café

Portland's Stumptown Coffee Roasters

Overview: Renowned Portland coffee store Stumptown Coffee Roasters is well-known for its skillfully roasted beans and handcrafted coffee beverages. The café serves a variety of cold brews, espresso cocktails, and single-origin coffees that are all expertly made. The sophisticated yet laid-back atmosphere makes it a favorite hangout for coffee lovers.

- Depending on size and kind, a coffee or espresso drink might cost anywhere from $4 to $8.

- **Directions**: 128 SW 3rd Ave, Portland, OR 97204 is the address. Pioneer Courthouse Square is just a short stroll (about five minutes) from downtown Portland. Alternatively, walk approximately 7 minutes north after using the MAX Light Rail to the Pioneer Courthouse/SW 6th stop.

Donuts Blue Star - Portland

Renowned Portland doughnut store Blue Star Donuts is renowned for its creative and upscale flavors. A variety of distinctive donuts, such as the Vanilla Bean Bourbon, Raspberry Bourbon Buttermilk, and Passion Fruit Cocoa Nib, are available, all crafted with premium ingredients. The donuts are well-known for their rich flavors and fluffy texture, and the shop has a modern style.

- The price per donut varies from $3 to $5, based on taste.

- **How to Get There**: 1155 SW Washington St., Portland, OR 97205 is the address. Pioneer Courthouse Square is ten minutes' walk from Portland's downtown. Alternatively, walk approximately five minutes east after using the MAX Light Rail to the Pioneer Courthouse/SW 6th stop.

Chapter 11. Options for Accommodation

opulent resorts

Newberg's Allison Inn & Spa

Situated in the center of Oregon's wine region, The Allison Inn & Spa provides an opulent haven with breathtaking views of the surrounding vineyards. The resort has exquisite accommodations, a top-notch spa, and a fine-dining restaurant with an emphasis on regional cuisine. Wine tastings, narrated vineyard excursions, and lounging by the outdoor pool are available to guests.

- **Cost**: Depending on the time of year and the style of the hotel, rates start at about $500 per night.

- **How to Get There**: From Portland, the Allison Inn & Spa is roughly a 40-minute drive to the southwest. To get to Newberg, travel I-5 S and OR-99W S. Portland International Airport (PDX), the closest airport, is about a 45-minute drive away from the resort.

Gleneden Beach's Salishan Coastal Lodge

With views of Siletz Bay and the Pacific Ocean, Salishan Coastal Lodge is a tranquil getaway situated on Oregon's stunning central coast. The lodge has a spa, an indoor pool, a golf course, and roomy accommodations. It offers the ideal starting point for visiting neighboring beaches, hiking routes, and coastal landmarks.

- **Cost**: Depending on the season and kind of accommodation, rates start at about $250 per night.

- **How to Get There**: Salishan Coastal Lodge may be reached by car from Portland about two hours to the west. Follow US-101 S to Gleneden Beach after taking US-26 W to US-101 S. Portland International Airport (PDX), the closest major airport, is approximately two hours drive away from the lodge.

Low-Cost Hotels

Portland Downtown Motel 6

Right in the middle of Portland, Motel 6 Portland Downtown provides lodging at an affordable price. Basic, spotless rooms with free Wi-Fi and free coffee in the lobby are available at the hotel. For tourists looking for ease and affordability, it's an easy decision.

- **Cost**: Between $80 and $120 per night.

How to Travel There:

- By automobile, from Portland International Airport: approximately fifteen minutes. Proceed to the downtown exit by following the signage after taking I-205 S to I-84 W.

- **From Portland Union Station**: A 20-minute walk or roughly 10 minutes by vehicle.

Portland Airport Econo Lodge
The reasonably priced Econo Lodge Portland Airport provides easy access to Portland International Airport throughout your stay. It offers free breakfast, free Wi-Fi, free airport transportation, and simple, comfortable accommodations. This is a sensible option for those who require easy access to the airport.

- **Cost**: About $120 to $130 per night.

How to Travel There:

- By automobile, from Portland International Airport: approximately five minutes. Take NE Airport Way, as directed by the airport departure signage, and make a right turn onto NE 82nd Ave. You'll see the hotel on your right.

- By automobile, from Portland Union Station: roughly 20 minutes. Take I-205 N from I-84 E, then get off at Airport Way.

Cozy Campsites and Cabins

Comfortable Cabins

Woods Edge Resort - Mount Hood
Situated at an elevation of 6,000 feet on the southern flanks of Mount Hood, Timberline Lodge provides a quaint and traditional mountain hideout.

A National Historic Landmark, the lodge is well-known for its magnificent vistas, year-round skiing and snowboarding, and exquisite alpine architecture. It transforms into a snowy paradise in the winter and offers hiking routes and outdoor activities in the summer. With its handcrafted wooden furnishings and stone fireplaces, the lodge's interior design combines luxury and rustic elements to create a warm and inviting ambiance for guests.

Price:

- Depending on the season and style of the hotel, rates start at about $200 per night.

How to Travel There:

- Drive US-26 E for 1.5 hours (approximately 60 miles) to Mount Hood from Portland. Follow the signs to Timberline Lodge Road, which takes you straight to the lodge.

Campsite at Lost Creek, Crater Lake National Park

Tent campers seeking a more private setting amid the wilderness will find Lost Creek Campground, a small, rustic campsite inside Crater Lake National Park, to be perfect. The campground is conveniently close to hiking trails and scenic vistas, and Crater Lake's breathtaking blue waters are only a short drive away. It is tucked away in the trees to the east of the lake. For those looking for some quiet time and a closer relationship with the park's natural splendor, this is a serene location.

Price:

- At Lost Creek, a night's camping typically costs about $10. Seasonally open, it's usually open from mid-June until early October.

How to Travel There:
Travel Highway 62 to the Crater Lake National Park's south gate to get to Lost Creek Campground. Proceed towards East Rim Drive by following the signs. The Phantom Ship Overlook is roughly three miles east of the campground. About four hours and 250 miles make up the travel from Portland to Crater Lake.

Campsites

Campground at Silver Falls State Park - Sublimity
Silver Falls State Park, renowned for its breathtaking waterfalls and verdant, woodland surroundings, is one of Oregon's most picturesque locations. The campground provides access to kilometers of hiking trails, including the well-known Trail of Ten Falls, where you may hike behind multiple waterfalls. It offers both tent and RV sites. The park is a nature lover's paradise, providing chances for hiking, wildlife viewing, and photography in a serene, unspoiled environment.

Price:

- Depending on the kind of site (tent or RV), camping at Silver Falls State Park costs between $24 and $31 per night. For additional vehicles, there can be additional costs.

How to Travel There:

- About 25 miles east of Salem, Oregon, is Silver Falls State Park. Take Highway 22 east from Salem, then make a left onto Highway 214 and follow the park's signage. It takes around 1.5 hours (about 60 miles) to drive from Portland to the campground, which is designated within the park.

Campground at Moulton Falls Regional Park - Yacolt

Nestled along the East Fork of the Lewis River lies Moulton Falls Regional Park, a picturesque haven. Beautiful waterfalls, pristine swimming holes, and charming hiking paths—including one that leads to the famed Moulton Falls Bridge—can all be found in the park. It's a fantastic place for nature enthusiasts to camp and take in the splendor of the Pacific Northwest because of the surrounding lush forests and tranquil rivers. The campground provides guests with a serene, unspoiled experience despite its rustic appearance.

Price:

- The cost of camping in Moulton Falls Regional Park varies from $20 to $25 a night, contingent upon the time of year and space available.

How to Travel There:

- About 45 miles northeast of Portland, Oregon, is Moulton Falls Regional Park, which is close to Yacolt, Washington. To get to the park, drive I-5 north to Exit 11 in Portland, then head north on NE 219th Street and NE Lucia Falls Road. The drive takes about sixty minutes.

Chapter 12. Family-Friendly Activities

Zoos and museums

Museums

Portland, Oregon: Portland Art Museum

One of the oldest art museums on the West Coast, the Portland Art Museum features a varied collection that is representative of many places and eras. Exhibits include Asian art, European masters, modern art, and Native American artifacts are available for visitors to view. In addition, the museum features graphic arts, photography, and changing shows that feature both regional and internationally recognized artists.

Price:

- $25 for adults

- **Elderly (62 and over)**: $22

- **Pupils**: $22

- **Children (17 and under)**: No charge

- Every month on the first Thursday from 5 to 8 p.m., admission is free.

How to Travel There:

The museum may be found at 1219 SW Park Ave. in Portland's downtown. Using public transportation to get there is simple. You may walk for roughly five minutes after taking the MAX

Light Rail to the Pioneer Square stop. Bus lines 6, 14, and 15 make neighboring stops as well. There is an extra charge for parking at adjacent garages.

Portland's Oregon Museum of Science and Industry (OMSI)

For those who enjoy science at all ages, the Oregon Museum of Science and Industry (OMSI) is an intriguing place to visit. OMSI provides an exciting learning experience with interactive exhibits spanning topics including technology, space, natural sciences, and the environment. The USS Blueback submarine, an IMAX theater, and planetarium performances are among the attractions. Regular rotation of special displays keeps the information interesting and new. Children's and adult interactive laboratories are also available at the museum.

Price:

- **Adults**: $15 (14–62)

- **Children (3–13)**: $10

- **Seniors (above 63)**: $12

- **Tour of the USS Blueback submarine**: extra $9

- **Tickets for the theater and planetarium**: extra expense

How to Travel There:

OMSI may be found in Portland at 1945 SE Water Ave. Buses and the Portland Streetcar are two forms of public transit. You can ride bus routes 6, 19, and 17 or take the MAX Light Rail to the OMSI/SE Water Ave stop. For a nominal cost, parking is offered on the premises.

Zoos

Portland's Oregon Zoo

With more than 1,800 animals spanning more than 230 species, including endangered species from around the globe, the Oregon Zoo is one of Portland's best family attractions. Elephant Lands, home to the renowned herd of Asian elephants at the zoo, Predators of the Serengeti, home to lions and cheetahs, and Pacific Shores, home to sea otters, seals, and penguins, are just a few of the habitats that guests can visit. Additionally, a section devoted to Northwest wildlife is there, featuring native animals such as the bald eagle and black bear.

The zoo is a year-round attraction with interactive exhibits, a kids' farm, and seasonal events like ZooLights during the holidays.

Price:

- **Adults (ages 12-64):** $24.

- **Seniors (above 65):** $21

- **Children (3–11):** $19.

- **Under 2:** No charge

How to Travel There:
4001 SW Canyon Rd. in Portland is the address of the Oregon Zoo. The Red or Blue Line of the MAX Light Rail can be used to travel to the Washington Park station, which is the closest station to the zoo. As an alternative, parking is offered on-site for $2 per hour.

Eugene's Cascades Raptor Center
For those who are interested in birds of prey, the Cascades Raptor Center in Eugene is a must-visit, a haven for wildlife lovers. Raptors including hawks, eagles, owls, and falcons are the main emphasis of this wildlife hospital and education facility's rehabilitation program. Through interactive exhibits and instructive displays, visitors can explore more than fifty resident birds in roomy outdoor enclosures, learning about the many species and their roles in the ecosystem.

These amazing birds, many of which have been saved and rehabilitated but are unable to be returned to the wild, will be up close and personal with you. Questions can be answered by the educated staff, and organized special events like educational seminars and live bird presentations are offered.

Price:

- **Adults**: $12

- **Seniors**: $10

- **Children (4–12)**: $6

- **Kids under 4**: No charge

How to Travel There:
The address of the Cascades Raptor Center is 32275 Fox Hollow Rd. in Eugene. It's roughly a fifteen-minute drive from downtown Eugene's downtown. There aren't many options for public transit, thus driving is advised. There is free on-site parking.

Parks with Themes and Outdoor Attractions

Families, adventure seekers, and lovers of the great outdoors will find something to enjoy in Oregon's many theme parks and outdoor activities. Here is a list of some popular locations along with transportation options:

Turner's Enchanted Forest Theme Park
Featuring fairy-tale-themed attractions including Storybook Lane, the Ice Mountain Bobsled Roller Coaster, and the Big Timber Log Ride, Enchanted Forest is a fanciful family-friendly park. Perfect for kids and anyone looking for a throwback experience.

- **How to Get There**: South of Salem, off of I-5. Take I-5 South to Exit 253 from Portland, then follow the park's instructions.

- **Price**: $16.95 for adults, $14.95 for kids aged 3 to 12, free for kids under three.

Portland's Oaks Amusement Park
A vintage amusement park with roller coasters, mini-golf, and other attractions located along the Willamette River in history. Renowned for its quaint, vintage vibe and welcoming environment for families.

- **How to Get There:** Portland's address is 7805 SE Oaks Park Way. Reached by taking I-84 East to 39th Ave. and then following the park's signage.

- **Cost**: Ride wristband costs vary according to height and day of the week, from $22.95 to $39.95.

Government Camp's Mount Hood Adventure Park is located at Skibowl.

This adventure park has summertime attractions like mountain biking, zip-lining, and alpine slides. In the winter, it becomes a snowy paradise with snowboarding, skiing, and snow tubing.

- **How to Get There**: Government Camp is located at 87000 E Government Camp Loop. Take US-26 East to the Government Camp exit from Portland.

- **Cost**: Wristbands for Adventure Parks start at $49. Tickets for the Alpine Slide cost $18 per ride.

Winston's Wildlife Safari

a 600-acre drive-through park where guests may get up close and personal with lions, giraffes, zebras, and elephants. An unforgettable encounter for lovers of animals.

How to Get There: 1790 Safari Road, Winston, is the address. Take Exit 119 off of I-5 South to Highway 42 East, then proceed to the park by following the signs.

Cost: $19 for children (3–12), $25 for adults.

Newport's Oregon Coast Aquarium

This aquarium has displays of marine life, such as sharks, octopuses, and sea otters. Spectacular vistas of marine life can be seen in the underwater passageways.

- **Directions**: 2820 SE Ferry Slip Rd, Newport is the address. Take US-101 South to Newport from Portland.

- Adults pay $24.95; children (3–12) pay $19.95.

Sublimity at Silver Falls State Park
This park, well-known for its "Trail of Ten Falls," offers a picturesque 7.2-mile trip where you may stroll behind waterfalls, have a picnic, and take in the scenery.

- **How to Get There**: 20024 Silver Falls Hwy SE, Sublimity is the address. To reach the park entrance, use Highway 22 East from Salem to Silver Falls Highway and then follow the instructions.

- **Cost**: $5 per day for parking.

Chapter 13. Day Outings & Adventures

The dunes of Oregon

Stretching over 40 miles along Oregon's southern coast, the Oregon Dunes National Recreation Area offers a wide variety of outdoor activities, picturesque scenery, and expansive areas of dunes. The dunes are an exceptional natural feature with magnificent, rolling patterns made of sand sculpted by the wind. Activities available to visitors include hiking, animal viewing, and dune buggy excursions.

Things to Look Into:

- **Dune Buggy and ATV Rides**: For an exciting adventure, explore the vast dunes in off-road vehicles.

- **Hiking Trails:** Paths such as the John Dellenback Dunes Trail provide breathtaking vistas and a chance to explore the region's varied flora and fauna.

- **Florence and the Coastline**: The town of Florence, which is close by, offers more attractions like views of the coast and the Siuslaw National Forest.

How to Travel There:

- From Portland, head south on I-5 to US-101. After arriving in Florence via US-101, proceed to the Oregon Dunes National Recreation Area by following the signs.

- From Eugene, travel US-101 North via OR-126 West. Go to Florence on US-101, and then continue to the Oregon Dunes.

Time of Travel:

- **From Portland**: About two and a half hours.

- **From Eugene**: About one and a half hours.

Price:

- **Entry Fee**: Free in most places; there may be a fee for some particular activities or park amenities. Depending on the company and length of the excursion, dune buggy rentals and guided tours can cost anywhere from $50 to $150.

The Oregon Dunes are a must-see location on the Oregon coast because they provide a unique encounter that combines the excitement of outdoor sports with the peace of nature.
Silver Falls State Park

Renowned for its breathtaking waterfalls, verdant forests, and picturesque hiking routes, Silver Falls State Park is situated near Sublimity, Oregon. The walk of Ten Falls, a 7.2-mile loop walk that passes by waterfalls that range in height from 27 to 178 feet, passes by ten significant waterfalls in the park.

Things to Look Into:
The famous Trail of Ten Falls provides beautiful vistas of ten waterfalls, including South Falls, which features a striking water curtain.

- **North Falls**: A shorter stroll will bring you to this lovely waterfall with a broad, cascading flow.

- **Silver Brook Falls**: Views of the waterfall as it cascades into the brook below are available from a picturesque overlook.

- **Wildlife and Flora**: The park is a haven for nature lovers, with a wide range of animal and plant species.

How to Travel There:
To get to Silver Falls State Park from Portland, take I-5 South to OR-22 East and then follow the signage.

- To get to the park from Eugene, take I-5 North to OR-22 East and then follow the signage.

Time of Travel:

- It takes roughly one hour and fifteen minutes from Portland.

- **From Eugene**: About one hour and fifteen minutes.

Price:

- **Day Use Fee:** $5 per car for parking during the day.

- **Camping fees**: Depending on the season and type of site, typical campsites cost $20 to $30 per night.

Mount St. Helens (border with Washington)
One of the most well-known volcanoes in the country, Mount St. Helens is situated directly across the border between

Washington and Oregon. It gained notoriety in 1980 after its devastating eruption. Presently, the volcano is a component of the Mount St. Helens National Volcanic Monument, providing tourists with an opportunity to investigate the striking terrain, gain knowledge about volcanic activity, and observe the tenacity of nature.

Things to Look Into:
Johnston Ridge Observatory: This visitor center offers ranger-led programs, breathtaking views of the crater, and educational exhibits regarding the 1980 eruption. The crater and lava dome are visible up close.

Hiking paths: Take a hike along one of the many paths, such as the Boundary Trail, which provides sweeping views of the surrounding blast zone, or the Hummocks Trail, which meanders through the eruption's debris field.

- **Spirit Lake**: See how this once-devastated lake is healing, even though it still has hundreds of fallen trees from the eruption.

  One of the longest lava tubes in the United States, Ape Cave provides a distinctive subterranean trekking experience.

How to Travel There:
To get to the Mount St. Helens Visitor Center or Johnston Ridge Observatory from Portland, take I-5 North and then follow the directions to WA-504 East, also known as the Spirit Lake Memorial Highway.

Travel I-5 South to WA-504 East from Seattle.
Time of Travel:

- Approximately one hour and forty-five minutes from Portland.

- It takes about two hours and thirty minutes from Seattle.

Price:

- Admission to Johnston Ridge Observatory is $8 per person (under 15 free).

- **Parking**: A Northwest Forest Pass or a $5 day-use fee may be needed at certain trailheads and recreation locations.

Section 14. Useful Travel Advice

Oregon transportation

Rental Automobiles

One of the greatest ways to experience Oregon's many landscapes—from the picturesque coastlines to the untamed mountains and energetic cities—is with a rental car. Hertz, Enterprise, and Avis are just a few of the well-known car rental companies that have locations in major cities, downtown districts, and airports like Eugene Airport and Portland International Airport. Road vacations are more flexible when you rent a car, especially if you want to drive across the Cascade Mountains or explore the Oregon Coast via Route 101.

Routes: Well-traveled routes include the Pacific Highway (Route 101), which hugs the coast, the picturesque I-84 Columbia River Gorge drive, and routes that pass through Crater Lake National Park and the Willamette Valley.

Terminals: Rental car companies are located downtown in Portland, Bend, and Salem, as well as at airports including Eugene, Medford, and Portland International (PDX), as well as Eugene, EUG, and MFR.

Cost: Depending on the type of vehicle and the time of year, car rentals in Oregon typically cost between $40 and $100 a day. Weekly rentals frequently qualify for discounts.

Public transportation (Portland's Trimet)

Portland's public transportation system, known as TriMet, offers an extensive and practical means of getting around the city and its environs. TriMet provides inexpensive and environmentally friendly transit throughout the Portland metro region by operating streetcars, light rail (MAX), and buses.

Routes: Portland International Airport (PDX), downtown Portland, Beaverton, and Gresham are all connected by the MAX Light Rail system. The Portland Streetcar makes loops through the downtown region, Pearl District, and South Waterfront, while the bus network serves the entire city, including the suburbs and neighborhoods.

Terminals: Pioneer Courthouse Square (Downtown), Beaverton Transportation Center (West Portland), and Gateway Transit Center (East Portland) are important transportation hubs. Major shopping centers, residential neighbourhoods, and landmarks are all conveniently close to MAX stations.

Cost: A single adult ticket on buses, MAX, and streetcars is $2.50, good for 2.5 hours of unlimited travel. Five dollars gets you a day pass. Reduced rates for youth and seniors are $1.25 for 2.5 hours and $2.50 for a full-day pass.

Buses
In Oregon, buses are an affordable and practical mode of transportation, especially in larger cities like Portland. Buses are an essential component of the public transportation system in the Portland metro region, where they are run by TriMet.

Routes: Beaverton, Gresham, Hillsboro, and other neighboring cities are all served by TriMet buses, which travel the whole Portland region. The #4 (Division/Fessenden), #12 (Barbur/Sandy), and #20 (Burnside/Stark) are popular routes that link downtown with surrounding areas and offer access to dining, shopping, and outdoor attractions. Additionally, the bus system and MAX Light Rail are integrated, making transfers simple.

Terminals: Pioneer Courthouse Square in downtown Portland, Beaverton Transit Center in West Portland, and Gateway Transit Center in East Portland are some of the main bus terminals and hubs. These hubs facilitate smooth transitions between different forms of transportation by connecting several bus lines with light rail.

Cost: A single adult ticket on the bus is $2.50; it is good for transfers to other buses, MAX, and streetcars, and it is valid for 2.5 hours. Five dollars gets you a day pass. Riders 65 years of age and older can purchase a $ 2.50-day pass or a $1.25 2.5-hour pass.

Amtrak
Amtrak offers a convenient and visually appealing means of transportation across Oregon and beyond, with well-maintained routes linking major cities and areas.

Routes: Portland and Salem are major stops on the Amtrak Cascades route, which runs from Eugene, Oregon, to Vancouver, British Columbia. For individuals who are going between Oregon and Washington, this route is excellent. The Coast Starlight route offers breathtaking views of the Pacific coast, the Cascade Range, and forested landscapes as it travels from Los Angeles to Seattle, including stops in Klamath Falls, Eugene, Portland, and other Oregon communities.

Terminals: Portland Union Station (800 NW 6th Ave, Portland); Eugene Station (433 Willamette St, Eugene); Salem Station (500 13th St SE, Salem); and Klamath Falls Station (1600 Oak Ave, Klamath Falls) are the state's principal Amtrak terminals. The biggest station in the state, Portland Union Station has dining options, lounges, and bathrooms.

Cost: Ticket costs differ according to the route, time of purchase, and kind of seats. For instance, a coach class one-way ticket from Portland to Eugene costs approximately $25–40, and a ticket from Portland to Seattle costs approximately $35–$60. Longer voyages, such as the Coast Starlight from Portland to Los Angeles, have coach seat fares starting at about $100.

Travel Safety and Protocols

Although Oregon is recognized for its warm and inviting environment, it's crucial to observe general safety precautions and travel politely to guarantee a pleasant and uneventful stay.

Safety Advice

Outdoor Safety: From mountains to beaches, Oregon boasts a wealth of natural attractions. Always keep an eye on your surroundings, have enough water on hand, and carry a map when trekking or exploring the outdoors. Verify the weather and notify someone of your plans, especially if you're going somewhere far from civilization, like a national park or forest.

Wildlife Awareness: Although seeing wildlife might be thrilling, keep in mind that some parts of Oregon are home to animals like cougars and bears. When camping, keep a safe distance, don't feed wildlife, and store food correctly to keep animals away.

Road Safety: Some of Oregon's highways are small and twisting, especially along the picturesque Pacific Highway (Route 101). Drive carefully through mountainous locations, and make sure your car is ready for snow and icy conditions in the winter. Drive cautiously and turn on your headlights.

Urban Safety: Take standard measures against urban hazards in places like Portland and Eugene, including staying away from dimly lit areas after dark and locking up personal goods. The cities of Oregon are typically safe, but like with any urban location, you should always be careful of your surroundings.

Natural Disasters: In some regions of the state, Oregon is particularly vulnerable to landslides, wildfires, and earthquakes. When it comes to wildfire season, remain up to date on local conditions, abide by park standards, and be mindful of evacuation routes while staying close to areas that are prone to wildfires.

Travel Protocols

Respect Nature: Since Oregon is known for its stunning natural surroundings, it is crucial to abide by the "Leave No Trace" philosophy. This includes keeping to designated pathways, packing out everything you bring in, and avoiding upsetting any wildlife or vegetation.

Environmental Consciousness: People in Oregon care about the environment. When traveling, think about renting an electric or hybrid car, taking public transportation, and bringing as little single-use plastic as possible. Because the state has a comprehensive recycling program, recycle whenever you can.

Outdoor Etiquette: Keep a calm environment whether you're hiking, camping, or at the seashore. Reduce your volume, show consideration for other hikers on the path, and stay away from disturbing wildlife. Make sure the parks and beaches are kept clean by disposing of your rubbish appropriately.

Local customs: Native American tribes and a robust environmental movement are among the varied cultures that call Oregon home. Be mindful of the customs and cultures of the area. When interacting with people, show them courtesy and consideration, and keep in mind that some natural sites may hold spiritual or cultural value.

Cycling Safety: Portland, in particular, in Oregon, is a bike-friendly state. When driving, keep an eye out for bikers, particularly in cities with bike lanes. Always make sure before opening a car door to prevent collisions with bicyclists who are passing.

Putting Together Essentials for Each Season

Because of the different landscapes and unpredictable weather in Oregon, thoughtful packing is essential for a relaxing and pleasurable journey. This guide will assist you in getting ready for any season, be it winter, spring, summer, or fall.

Winter: January to February
Weather: chilly with snow and rain, with the mountains and eastern Oregon having the most of it. Areas around the coast are wetter yet milder.

Essentials

Waterproof Outerwear: During Oregon's rainy season, a robust, insulated waterproof jacket is essential for staying warm and dry.
Layered Clothes: Bring layers to adapt to changing indoor and outdoor temperatures, such as fleece, sweaters, and thermal shirts.

Waterproof Boots: Waterproof boots with good traction will shield you from rain, snow, and ice whether you're trekking or just strolling through towns.

Warm Accessories: If you're heading to the mountains for skiing or snowshoeing, pack hats, gloves, scarves, and wool socks to remain warm.

Travel Umbrella: When visiting cities, a small, wind-resistant umbrella comes in handy.
Lip balm and moisturizers: The dry winter air can cause dryness on your skin and lips.

Springtime (April-May)

Weather: Lots of rain, cool to moderate temps, and flowering flowers.

Essentials

Rain Gear: In Oregon, springtime frequently brings showers. It's imperative to have a lightweight rain jacket or poncho.

Light Layers: Because the weather can vary quickly from sunny spells to showers, dress in light layers like cardigans and long-sleeved shirts.

Comfortable Shoes: For visiting cities and natural paths, sneakers or waterproof walking shoes are great options.

Sunglasses: Even in the spring, sunny days in Oregon may be intense, so carry a pair with you.

Compact Backpack: Ideal for day travels, it can hold water, food, and any extra clothing you take off.

Binoculars: Perfect for observing birds in parks and marshes, particularly in the spring when they migrate.

August to June is summer.

Weather: Dry and warm to hot, especially in the state's eastern and inland regions.
Essentials

Light, Breathable Clothes: For hot summer days, bring t-shirts, shorts, and airy dresses made of breathable materials like cotton or linen.

Sun Protection: Especially at high altitudes or along the coast, sunscreen, sunglasses, and a wide-brimmed hat are essentials for shielding oneself from the sun.

Swimwear: Bring your bathers for journeys to Oregon's rivers, lakes, and waterfalls, as well as for beach days along the coast.

Sandals or trekking Shoes: Bring comfortable sandals for days when you're not going to be trekking and sturdy shoes if you will be hiking.

Reusable Water Bottle: Drink plenty of water when traveling, particularly in arid and hotter regions like southern Oregon or the high desert.

Insect repellent is essential for trekking and camping to keep mosquitoes and ticks away from you.

Autumn (September through November)

Weather: mild and chilly, with the beginning of the rainy season in late fall and changing leaves.

Essentials

Layered Outfits: Because the weather can change from balmy afternoons to chilly evenings, bring lightweight sweaters, long sleeves, and jackets that can be layered.
Waterproof Boots or Shoes: Waterproof footwear is vital because fall can bring rainy weather, particularly in the valleys and along the shore.

Rain Jacket: Since autumn temperatures are frequently mild, a lightweight raincoat will keep you dry without overheating.

Jeans or hiking pants: Sturdy and comfy for strolling through cities or doing light hiking in the woods.

A light scarf or beanie can keep you warm when the wind picks up, especially in coastal or higher-altitude regions.

All-Year Essentials

Camera or Smartphone: The state of Oregon is always quite photogenic, so bring along a nice camera or phone that has lots of storage.

Map/Guidebook: If you're traveling through an area with spotty phone coverage, a decent offline map app or guidebook will come in handy for navigating the state's attractions.

Power Bank: During lengthy outdoor activities or road vacations, keep your gadgets charged.

Reusable Tote Bag: Since Oregon is a green state, you'll frequently need to bring your bag when you go shopping.

Chapter 15. Final Thoughts

Oregon's Undiscovered Treasures

While Crater Lake and Mount Hood are two of Oregon's most well-known tourist destinations, the state is also home to several lesser-known but no less breathtaking hidden jewels that provide unforgettable experiences away from the masses.

Blue Pool at Tamolitch

What to Explore: Tamolitch Blue Pool is a stunning natural pool that is well-known for its very vivid blue hue. It is situated along the McKenzie River Trail in the Willamette National Forest. The pool is situated in a picturesque rocky bowl surrounded by lush flora and is supplied by underground springs. The extremely cold water discourages swimming, but the pool is a great place to take pictures, have a picnic, and observe the surrounding scenery. The McKenzie River Trail, which is close by, offers possibilities for trekking through old-growth forests, seeing wildlife, and soaking in the tranquil environment of Oregon's wilderness. The surrounding area offers a tranquil getaway.

Trekking:
There is a moderate difficulty level to the 4-mile round-trip climb to Tamolitch Blue Pool.

You'll follow the McKenzie River Trail, which offers beautiful vistas of the forest, tiny rapids, and waterfalls along sections of the trail that run beside the river.

Price:

- The site is free to see, however parking at the trailhead costs about $5.

- Parking may require a Northwest Forest Pass, which may be bought online or from local vendors.

How to Travel There:

Travel approximately sixty miles east on OR-126 toward McKenzie Bridge from Eugene.
The Tamolitch Blue Pool Trailhead, close to Trail Bridge Reservoir, is where you'll find the trailhead, which is right off Highway 126.
From Eugene, the travel takes about one hour and fifteen minutes.

Beds of Fossil John Day

What to Explore: Preserving millions of years' worth of plant and animal fossils, the John Day Fossil Beds National Monument is a rare location that provides a peek into Earth's ancient past. There are three sections to the monument:

The Painted Hills Unit is well-known for its vividly colored hills composed of layers of claystone and volcanic ash. It offers several hiking paths where visitors may discover the area's rich geological past and take in the breathtaking scenery.

The Thomas Condon Paleontology Center is located in the Sheep Rock Unit. It offers guided tours, fossil displays, and a functional laboratory where paleontologists prepare specimens for study.

The towering rock formations and prehistoric fossils embedded in the cliffs of Clarno Unit are its main features. Hiking the Clarno Arch Trail is a quick but beautiful way to see these natural marvels.

Numerous interpretive paths that offer a view into various eras of Earth's history and the fossils found in the area are available at the monument. For those who want to learn more about Oregon's prehistoric landscape, there are educational programs, guided tours, and self-directed walks available.

Price:

- The John Day Fossil Beds National Monument does not charge admission.

- There are no trail or parking fees, but donations are accepted to support park maintenance.

How to Travel There:

- From Bend, travel north on US-97 and then east on OR-26. The trip is roughly 130 kilometers long and takes about 2.5 hours.

- Travel east on I-84 to Biggs Junction from Portland, then turn south on US-97 and east on OR-26. It takes roughly 4 hours to complete the 220 miles of this route.

Alvord Desert

What to Explore: Known for its enormous, miles-long, fractured salt flats, the Alvord Desert is a lonely, dry region in southeast Oregon. It provides a calm, unearthly setting for travelers looking for adventure and seclusion. Important events and locations consist of:

The Salt Flats: It's great to explore the dry lake bed by bicycle, automobile, or foot. Activities available to visitors include photography, land sailing, off-roading, and hiking. A remarkable contrast is produced by the never-ending stretch of level, white land set against the backdrop of Steens Mountain, particularly at sunrise and sunset.

Hot Springs: After a day of exploring the desert, unwind in the neighboring Alvord Hot Springs. Privately run, the springs offer rustic pools overlooking the desert.

Stargazing: The Alvord Desert is a great place to see stars because of its isolation and absence of light pollution. A stunning picture of the night sky is provided by the Milky Way and innumerable stars visible in the pure desert skies.

Nature & Wildlife: Despite its arid appearance, the desert is home to a variety of desert animals, such as pronghorn antelope, wild mustangs, and raptors. There are additional chances to explore the Steens Mountain Wilderness, which offers hiking routes and alpine views, in the nearby locations.

Price:

- The desert is open for free.

- For day use, Alvord Hot Springs charges about $10 per person.

How to Travel There:

- Travel east on OR-78 from Burns, Oregon, and then turn south on Fields-Denio Road. It takes nearly two hours to complete the roughly 90-mile route.

- From Portland: Portland is located around 370 miles southeast of the Alvord Desert. It's a seven-hour drive, mostly on US-26 and OR-78.

The Opal Creek Wilderness

What You Can Explore: The Willamette National Forest is home to the breathtaking Opal Creek Wilderness. Hikers and lovers of the great outdoors will adore this place because of its waterfalls, emerald-green swimming holes, and old-growth forests. Highlights consist of:

Opal Pool: Surrounded by moss-covered rocks, this turquoise swimming hole is one of the main draws. It offers crystal-clear water. It's the ideal location to cool off on a sweltering summer day.

Hiking Trails: The Opal Creek Trail winds through old Douglas fir and cedar trees for a 6.5-mile round trip, leading to Jawbone Flats. A look into Oregon's logging and mining history can be had in Jawbone Flats, a historic mining hamlet.

Waterfalls: There are several picturesque waterfalls on the trail, such as Sawmill Falls, which drop into crystal-clear pools below.
Wildlife: The wilderness is a wonderful place to observe nature because it is home to a wide variety of wildlife, such as black bears, cougars, deer, and other bird species.

Price:

- Although parking at the trailhead needs a Northwest Forest Pass, which costs $5 per day or $30 for an annual pass, access to Opal Creek

- Wilderness is free.

How to Travel There:

- To get to OR-22 (Exit 253 toward Detroit Lake) from Portland, take I-5 south. Proceed east on OR-22, then make a left turn onto North Fork Road and proceed to Opal Creek by following the signage. The trip is around 85 miles long and takes about two hours.

- **From Salem**: Travelling 50 miles southeast on OR-22 and North Fork Road will take you around 1.5 hours.

Promoting Eco-Friendly Travel

Travel sustainably is becoming more and more crucial as more people discover Oregon's beauty to protect the state's natural areas and cultural legacy. In addition to being good for the environment, sustainable travel helps local communities and guarantees that future generations will be able to have the same experiences.

Cut Down on Your Environmental Impact

Reduce Waste: Bring shopping bags, utensils, and reusable water bottles. It's great to appreciate Oregon's breathtaking scenery litter-free, so make sure to always pack out what you bring in.

Select Eco-Friendly Transportation: Try to use walking, bicycling, or public transportation wherever you can. To cut down on pollution, think about renting electric or hybrid cars for long-distance travel. The effective Trimet system in Portland is an excellent means of sustainable city exploration.

Remain on Designated routes: To protect wildlife habitats and flora, hikers should always remain on designated routes.

Encourage Local Companies and Communities

Shop and Eat Locally: Encourage the growth of Oregon's economy by patronizing neighbourhood eateries, going to farmers' markets, and purchasing goods produced there. This lowers the carbon footprint of moving goods while keeping money in the local economy.

Respect Local Culture: Pay attention to cultural practices and show respect for the way of life of the people you are interacting with, whether you are in a small town or an indigenous community. A thorough understanding of Oregon's rich past enhances your trip experience.

Save Water and Energy

Reduce Water Use: Try to cut down on the amount of water you use by taking shorter showers and reusing towels in places where water supplies are limited. In Oregon, there are lots of eco-friendly lodging options that provide ways for you to save resources while visiting.

Energy Efficiency: When not in use, turn off air conditioning, lights, and devices. Choose green energy sources, like solar electricity, if your lodging has them, whenever you can.

Keep Wildlife and Natural Environments Safe

Leave No Trace: Adhere to the principles of Leave No Trace by being cautious not to impede wildlife migration, feed animals, or remove plants and rocks. When left undisturbed, Oregon's unique wildlife, which includes eagles in the forests and whales along the shore, thrives.

Engage in Conservation Efforts: A lot of Oregon's parks and wilderness areas have volunteer opportunities, clean-up days, and environmental education programs. Your participation helps to ensure that these areas remain open for longer.

Select Eco-Friendly Lodging Options

Select accommodations that put sustainability first, such as eco-lodges or establishments with green certificates. Utilizing techniques like recycling, composting, and energy efficiency, many Oregonian resorts and hotels aim to reduce their environmental effect.

Chapter 16. Beneficial Resources and Contacts

Centers for Tourist Information

Visitor Information Center in Portland

- Pioneer Courthouse Square is located in Portland, Oregon 97205 at 701 SW 6th Ave.

- Please call (503) 275-8355.

Visitors Association of the Oregon Coast

- **Address**: 186 E Olive St., 97365 Newport, OR

- Please call (541) 574-2679.

Visitor Center for Southern Oregon

- **Address**: 1314 Center Dr., 97501 Medford, OR

- Please call (541) 773-8227.

Bend Tourist Information

- The address is Suite 160, 750 NW Lava Road, Bend, OR 97703.

- Please call (541) 382-8048.

Cascades & Coast Visitor Center, Eugene

- **Location**: Eugene, OR 97401, 754 Olive St.

- **Get in touch**: (541) 484-5307

The Chamber of Commerce in the Astoria-Warrenton Area

- **Address**: 111 W Marine Dr., 97103 Astoria, Oregon

- Please call (503) 325-6311

Visitor Center in Crater Lake National Park

- **Location**: Crater Lake National Park, Rim Village Visitor Center, OR 97604

- Please call (541) 594-3000.

Contacts for Emergencies

All-purpose emergency (fire, police, ambulance):

- **Call**: 911

Assistance from Non-Emergency Police:

- **Call**: 311

State Police of Oregon:

- Please call (800) 442-0776.

Poison Control Division:

- **Call number**: (800) 222-1222

Roadside Help (AAA in Oregon and Idaho):
Dialing (800) 222-4357

Travel Information from the Oregon Department of Transportation (ODOT):

- **Phone**: (800) 977-6368 or (511).

Public health authority for Oregon:

- **Caller number**: (971) 673-1222

Coast Guard (for emergencies along the coast):

- In the Astoria Sector, call (503) 861-6211.

Crater Lake Emergency Number for the National Park Service:

- **Caller number**: (541) 594-3000

In the event of a forest or wilderness emergency, the US Forest Service
Phone (Pacific Northwest Region): (503) 808-2468

Websites and Apps for Travel

Official Website of Oregon Tourism:

- https://traveloregon.com

ODOT, the Oregon Department of Transportation:

- URL: tripcheck.com

TripCheck app (for real-time traffic updates and road conditions)

Airbnb:
- AirBnB.com is the website.

- **App**: Airbnb (for places to stay)

Hopper (Travel & Hotel Offers):

- Hopper.com is the website.

- Hopper app

Kayak (Bookings for Hotels, Cars, and Flights):

- Kayak.com is the website.

- Kayak app

AllTrails (Outdoor Recreation and Hiking):

- https://alltrails.com

- AllTrails app

State Parks in Oregon:

- Oregon State Parks' website

- **App**: State Parks Guide for Oregon

Google Maps (Info on Public Transportation and Navigation):

- Maps.google.com website

- Google Maps app

Yelp (Reviews and Restaurants):

- Yelp.com is the website.

- Yelp app

Roadtrippers: Arrange Beautiful Road Journeys

- https://roadtrippers.com

- Roadtrippers app

Photographers' Secrets for Seizing Gorgeous Moments in Oregon

Golden Hour Lighting:
Photograph at the golden hour, which is right before or right after sunrise. Warm, gentle light produces striking shadows and improves scenery.

When: Late afternoon and early morning.

Employ a Tripod:

Use a tripod to get crisp, steady pictures, especially during long exposures or in low light. It aids in removing camera wobble.

When: Taking pictures at night, in dim light, or while photographing landscapes.

Take control of the Oregon Coast:

Advice: To capture the vast magnificence of the coasts and striking cliffs, use a wide-angle lens. Waves can get a smooth look from prolonged exposure.

Location: Other coastal regions, including Seaside Beach and Cannon Beach.

Add Front-Color Elements:

Advice: You may add depth and dimension to your compositions by including intriguing foreground components. These could be flowers, rocks, or anything else that adds interest to the picture.

When: Pictures of scenery and wildlife.

Pay Attention to the Details:

Advice: Get up close and concentrate on small details, such as the sand's patterns, the textures of the leaves, or the elaborate architectural elements of the area.

When: Photographing urban nature or distinctive characteristics.

Make Use of Leading Lines
A helpful tip is to use man-made or natural lines (such as rivers, highways, or walkways) to draw the viewer's attention to the picture and give it a sense of depth.

When: Taking pictures of cities and landscapes.

Try Out a Composition Exercise:

Advice: To create a more dynamic composition, position your subject off-center using the rule of thirds. To get interesting images, don't be scared to try new things and defy the norm.

When: All forms of picture taking.

Catch Local Wildlife:
A telephoto lens can be used to take pictures of animals without upsetting them. The keys include knowing animal behavior and having patience.

Location: National parks and wildlife reserves.
Edit Cautiously:

A word of caution: While post-processing might improve your images, don't go overboard. To enhance the quality of your photos, make adjustments to brightness, contrast, and sharpness.

When: Right after you take your pictures.

Remain respectful and safe:

Advice: Always respect the environment and wildlife, and abide by local laws. Make sure you are safe when taking pictures, particularly in untamed or isolated areas.

When: For any animal and outdoor photos.
Greetings, Readers

Humble Request

The Ultimate Oregon Adventure. As a travel guide author, each page in this book captures not just the spirit of Oregon but also the result of many hours of study, exploration, and hard work. To ensure you fully enjoy this amazing state's charms, I've put my all into capturing its splendor, from the untamed coastline to the energetic metropolis.

Your suggestions and compliments are much appreciated. Not only do they offer support, but they also assist me in honing my skills so that I can supply you with even more comprehensive and insightful travel recommendations. Every review serves as a tribute to the time and money spent traveling to Oregon, guaranteeing that all of the information you read here is true and beneficial.

Your observations serve as a compass for me as a writer. You join a group of travelers who want to get the most out of their travels by contributing your ideas. In addition to helping me advance, your review helps other tourists see the finest that Oregon has to offer.

I appreciate you joining me on this journey. My work is motivated by your encouragement and criticism, and I sincerely appreciate your role in this continuing process.

Sincere regards,

Brandie Coleman

Made in the USA
Las Vegas, NV
19 November 2024

12098366R00066